CISTERCIAN FATHERS SERIES: NUMBER NINE

WILLIAM OF ST THIERRY

Volume Three

THE ENIGMA OF FAITH

CISTERCIAN FATHERS SERIES

Board of Editors

CISTERCIAN FATHERS SERIES: NUMBER NINE

THE WORKS OF
WILLIAM OF ST THIERRY

Volume Three

The Enigma of Faith

Translated, with an introduction and notes, by
John D. Anderson

CISTERCIAN PUBLICATIONS
CONSORTIUM PRESS
Washington, D.C.
1974

Cistercian Fathers Series   ISBN 0-87907-000-5
The Works of William of St Thierry ISBN 0-87907-300-4
This Volume   cloth   ISBN 0-87907-309-8
                     paper   ISBN 0-87907-709-3

Library of Congress Catalog Number: 74-4465

© Copyright, Cistercian Publications, Inc. 1973

Ecclesiastical permission to publish this book has been received from
Bernard Flanagan, Bishop of Worcester, December 4, 1972.

CONTENTS

ABBREVIATIONS

Adv Abl	William of St Thierry, *Disputatio adversus Petrum Abaelardum,* PL 180:249-328
Cant	William of St Thierry *Expositio super cantica canticorun,* SCh 82; tr. *Exposition on the Song of Songs,* CF 6.
CC	Corpus Christianorum, Series Latina (Turnhout: Brepols, 1945).
CF	Cistercian Fathers Series (Spencer, Mass., Washington, D.C.: Cistercian Publications, 1970).
CS	Cistercian Studies Series (Spencer, Mass., Washington, D.C.: Cistercian Publications, 1969).
CSEL	Corpus Scriptorum Ecclesiasticorum Latinorum (Vienna: Hoelder-Pïchler-Tempsky, 1866).
De doc. chr.	St Augustine, *De doctrina christiana,* CC 32:1-167; tr. *Christian Instruction,* FC 2:1-235.
De trin.	St Augustine, *De Trinitate libri XV,* CC 50-50A; tr. *The Trinity,* FC 45.
De vera rel.	St Augustine, *De vera religione,* CC 32:187-260.
Ep	Letter(s).
Er Guil	William of St Thierry, *De erroribus Guillelmi de Conchis,* PL 180:333-340.
Exp Rm	William of St Thierry, *Expositio in Epistolam ad Romanos,* PL 180:547-694.
FC	The Fathers of the Church (New York, Washington, D.C.: Catholic University of America Press, 1947).
PG	Patrologiae cursus completus, series Graeca (Paris, 1844-1855).
PL	Patrologiae cursus completus, series Latina (Paris, 1878-1890).
RTAM	*Recherches de théologie ancienne et médiévale* (Louvain, 1929).
SCh	Sources Chrétiennes (Paris: Cerf, 1943).
Spec fid	William of St Thierry, *Speculum fidei,* PL 180:365-398; tr. *The Mirror of Faith* (London: Mowbrays, 1959).
TLL	*Thesaurus linguae latinae* (Leipzig, 1900).

PREFACE

THIS VOLUME grew out of a doctoral dissertation submitted to the Catholic University of America in October, 1971, entitled *The Enigma fidei of William of Saint Thierry, a Translation and Commentary*. The present work embodies a substantial reworking of the introductory material, notes, and the translation itself of that dissertation.

The translation is based on a reading of the only twelfth-century manuscript of the *Enigma* extant, Charleville MS 114, and an examination of the fifteenth-century manuscript, Uppsala C. 79. Facsimiles of these manuscripts were provided by the Managing Editor of the Cistercian Fathers Series, M. Basil Pennington.

The notes provided in this volume have been formulated for the general reader, for the most part. More extensive commentary with exact references to original sources can be found in my dissertation mentioned above.

I wish to express my appreciation to the Editors of the Cistercian Fathers Series for accepting my work for publication. Special thanks are due to Fr Pennington for his constant assistance.

John D. Anderson

INTRODUCTION

WILLIAM OF ST THIERRY: LIFE AND WORKS

SINCE OTHER VOLUMES IN THIS SERIES present an exposition of the life of William of St Thierry, some apology seems necessary for the following pages.[1] This brief section on the life of William has a double purpose: a demonstration of the tentative and hypothetical nature of some of the facts and chronology presently associated with the life of William; an indication of what is known about William's life. An outline of the events of the life of William of St Thierry is possible, but serious problems arise when an attempt is made to develop this outline into anything like a detailed *curriculum vitae*. In any event, the sources for William's life are six: his own writings; the Letters of St Bernard, especially from the Abbey of St Thierry; the necrologies of Signy and the Carthusian house of Mont Dieu (*Mons Dei*); the *Chronicle of Signy*, and finally, the anonymous *Vita antiqua* published by Albert Poncelet in 1908. The data provided by these documents, however, are relatively meager.

The most recent interpreters of these data are André Adam Jean-Marie Déchanet, and Jacques Hourlier.[2] These scholars are in basic agreement on their interpretation of the

1. See the Introduction in CF 3 by Jacques Hourlier OSB, pp. 3-35; also, Déchanet, *William of St Thierry, the Man and His Work* (Spencer, 1972) CS 10.

2. Included here should also be a recent dissertation: Stanislaus Ceglar, *William of Saint Thierry, the Chronology of His Life With a Study of His Treatise On the Nature of Love, His Authorship of the Brevis commentatio, the In Lacu, and the Reply to Cardinal Matthew* (Ann Arbor: University Microfilms, 1971).

1

traditional data and their structuring of a life of William of St Thierry. Nevertheless, there are several instances in their presentation of the historical data where they seem to be somewhat subjective. Hourlier's work on William's chronology is essentially derivative[3] and adds nothing to the work of Adam and Déchanet. Therefore, it is to these latter two scholars that some attention must be given.

The matter of establishing a birthdate for William is instructive for exemplifying the hypothetical nature of the work of Adam and Déchanet on some points of William's life. Adam places William's birth around the year 1090; he admits that the date of William's birth is not known, but due to the relationship between William and Bernard of Clairvaux, which Adam interpretes as a relationship between two men of equal age, he places William's birth around 1090.[4] It is interesting to note that André Wilmart rejects this date and places William's birth in 1080 because he believes William was older than his friend.[5] Déchanet rejects both these dates and, taking 1111 as his point of departure, places William's birth in 1085.[6] He feels that William was at Laon in 1111.[7] He has a theory that William and Abelard met at Laon while they were both students there.[8] Working backward from this date of 1111 Déchanet states that William of St Thierry was born in 1085.[9] When all is said and done the most precise dating of William's birth seems to be that of Poncelet, the editor of the anonymous *Vita antiqua*, during the last quarter of the eleventh century.[10]

3. Jacques Hourlier, trans. and ed., *La contemplation de Dieu, L'oraison de Dom Guillaume*, SC 61 (Paris, 1959) p. 7, n. 1. See also Houlier's Introduction in CF 3.

4. André Adam, *Guillaume de Saint-Thierry sa vie et ses oeuvres* (Bourg, 1923) p. 27.

5. André Wilmart, "La série et la date des ouvrages de Guillaume de Saint-Thierry," *Revue Mabillon* 14 (1924) p. 159, n. 2.

6. Jean Marie Déchanet, *William of St Thierry, the Man and His Work*, CS 10, (Spencer, 1972) p. 1, n. 2. Henceforth this book will be referred to as Déchanet, *William*.

7. *Ibid.*

8. See his "L'amitié d'Abélard et de Guillaume de Saint-Thierry," *Revue d'histoire ecclesiastique* 35 (1939) pp. 761-774.

9. Déchanet, *William*, p. 1, n. 2.

10. Albert Poncelet, "Vie ancienne de Guillaume de Saint-Thierry," *Mélanges Godefroid Kurth* (Paris, 1908) p. 85. Ceglar posits a still earlier date. See above, n. 2.

Adam and Déchanet are both somewhat effusive and fail to adhere to the limitations imposed by the lack of documentation on William's life. For example, on the question of whether William and his companion Simon studied at Reims or Laon, both scholars give questionable responses. Adam posits a completely unsubstantiated textual reconstruction to a lacuna in the text of the *Vita antiqua*.[11] It is this reconstruction which introduces our only mention of Anselm of Laon and the School of Laon in reference to William's place of study. Both Déchanet and Davy reject Adam's reconstruction as physically impossible in terms of the blank space on the manuscript.[12] Déchanet, nevertheless, goes on to say that William studied at Laon and confirms this by what he believes to be indisputable evidence: the influence of Laon and Anselm of Laon on William's works.[13] He says that William's writings embody the spirit which animated the School at Laon, its conception of theology, and its method of exegesis to such an extent that he was without doubt a student there.[14] Déchanet points out the great influence of the works of John Scotus Erigena at the School of Laon and William's own use of the works of Erigena. He then asks where William could have come to know the works of Erigena and his translations of the Greek Fathers if not at Laon.[15] This does not seem to give an historically sound answer to the problem. It might be pointed out that John R. Williams reads the data differently and concludes that whether William received his education at Reims in the period, 1105-1115, is an open question, but that our sole source of information, the *Vita antiqua*, certainly indicates that he did.[16] Furthermore, Williams is not convinced by the arguments of Déchanet that

11. Poncelet, *op. cit.*, p. 89. A discussion of the text and Adam's reconstruction can be found in Déchanet, *William* p. 2, n. 4.

12. Déchanet, *William* p. 2 n. 4; M.-M. Davy, *Un traité de la vie solitaire, Lettre Aux Frères du Mont-Dieu de Guillaume de Saint-Thierry* (Paris, 1940) pp. 16-19.

13. Déchanet, *William* pp. 2-3.

14. Déchanet, *William* p. 3.

15. *Ibid.*

16. John R. Williams, "The Cathedral School of Reims in the Time of Master Alberic, 1118-1136," *Traditio* 20 (1964) p. 95.

William of St Thierry's concept of theology and his method of exegesis were those of Anselm of Laon.[17] Moreover, he concludes that owing to the defective condition of the *Vita* we are unable to be certain that William and Simon were educated at the Cathedral School of Laon.[18]

This brief exposition of some of the shortcomings of modern scholars working on the life of William of St Thierry is meant to indicate a need for caution in dealing with their interpretations of the historical data about William. It remains to sketch a tentative life of William based on the factual evidence.

William was born at Liége of noble parentage,[19] sometime during the last quarter of the eleventh century.[20] With a companion, Simon, whom some authorities believe to be his brother,[21] William left Liège to study, apparently at Reims. This can be concluded from the *Vita*[22] and from the *Chronicle of Signy* which states that William was a well-educated man when he entered Signy.[23] After studying for some time[24] William and Simon entered the monastery of St Nicaise of Reims.[25] Simon later became abbot of St Nicolas-aux-Bois in the diocese of Laon and after a lengthy abbacy died at some unknown date.[26] Adam gives no date for the entry of William and Simon into St Nicaise, but speculates that it may have been in 1115, the year, he says, when Bernard of Clairvaux was ordained priest.[27] Likewise, Déchanet has no documenta-

---

17. Williams, *op. cit.,* p. 95 n. 14. Williams does not substantiate his position with any evidence; he simply states his opposition to Déchanet's opinion. See Déchanet, *William* p. 3 and pp. 135-153 for a discussion of William of St Thierry's theology.

18. Williams, *op. cit.,* p. 95.

19. Poncelet, *op. cit.,* p. 89.

20. Poncelet, *op. cit.,* p. 85.

21. Déchanet, *William* p. 5, n. 13.

22. Poncelet, *op. cit.,* p. 89.

23. Léopold Delisle, "Chronique de l'abbaye de Signy," *Bibliothèque de l'Ecole des Chartes* 55 (1894) p. 646.

24. Poncelet, *op. cit.* p. 89.

25. *Ibid.*

26. *Ibid.*

27. Adam, *op. cit.,* p. 25. Adam seems to base this date on the work of Vacandard in his *Vie de Saint Bernard* (Paris, 1897) Vol. 2, p. 66, n. 1.

ry evidence for their date of entry into St Nicaise, but working from the time he wishes William to have been at Laon (between 1111-1113) he concludes that 1113 was the date when William received the habit at St Nicaise.[28]

William was later elected abbot of St Thierry near Reims.[29] This occurred in 1119 or 1120.[30] This date can be determined from the fact that William's predecessor still governed the abbey in 1119;[31] also, William was abbot of St Thierry for fourteen years and five months according to a catalogue of abbots of St Thierry cited by Mabillon,[32] and his successor's signature is on a document of St Thierry for the year 1135.[33] The abbacy of William at St Thierry is praised in the *Vita antiqua* as a time of exemplary discipline and spiritual leadership.[34] During this time William's friendship with Bernard of Clairvaux developed. These two men had apparently met for the first time toward the end of 1118.[35] Eventually, William left St Thierry and became a Cistercian monk at the monastery of Signy in the diocese of Reims.[36] The monastery had been recently founded on March 25, 1134 according to the *Chronicle of Signy*.[37] The *Vita* says that

28. Déchanet, *William* p. 15, n. 1.
29. Poncelet, *op. cit.*, p. 89. The *Vita* describes the location of St Thierry as *locus urbi Remensi imminet*. The monastery is situated on Mont d'Hor about five miles northwest of Reims: see U. Chevalier, *Répertoire des sources historiques du moyen âge: topo-bibliographie* (Paris, 1903) Part 2, p. 2778.
30. For the date April, 1121 see Ceglar, *op. cit.*, p. 135.
31. *Gallia christiana* (Paris, 1751) Vol. 9, pp. 186-187.
32. PL 182:207D.
33. *Ibid.*
34. Poncelet, *op. cit.*, p. 90.
35. E. Vacandard, *Vie de Saint Bernard* (Paris, 1897) Vol. 1, pp. 76-77.
36. Signy is northwest of Reims, about five miles from the city of Rethel which is on the Aisne River; see F. van der Meer, *Atlas de l'Ordre Cistercien* (Paris, 1965) p. 297.
37. Delisle, *op. cit.*, p. 645 n. 5 and p. 659; also, see Adam, *op. cit.*, p. 59 where the author gives the date of March 20, 1135 for the founding. This is based on Janauschek, *Origines cistercienses* (Vienna, 1877) Vol. 1, p. 34 where it is said that the year 1134 is based on a system of computing years different from ours. However, it is uncertain what system of computation was in use in Reims in the twelfth century. Giry, *Manuel de Diplomatique* (Paris, 1894) p. 117 speaks of two systems, one beginning the year with Easter and one with the Annunciation (March 25). The former was in use in the tenth century and spread during the

William was drawn to the Cistercians by a desire for solitude and spiritual growth.[38] William had been contemplating this transfer from the Benedictines to the Cistercians for some time[39] and had mentioned it to St Bernard who counseled against it, feeling that William's mission was at St Thierry.[40] The date for William's arrival at Signy is either 1134 or 1135.[41] William was a monk at Signy until his death on September 8, 1147 or 1148.[42]

Sometime during his years at Signy William was weakened

---

eleventh. The latter, Giry says, was employed in the area of Reims during the twelfth century. Giry's source for this is the Maurist *L'Art de verifier les dates* (Paris, 1818) Vol. 6, p. 13 and 28. However, these pages speak of the eleventh and the thirteenth centuries, saying nothing of the twelfth. Moreover, Janauschek gives authorities for 1133 and 1134 in addition to his choice of 1135. Thus, the year seems uncertain; however, mention should be made of D. Hans Lietzmann, *Zeitrechnung* (Berlin, 1956) p. 128, which indicates that it was a Cistercian practice to begin the year with the Annunciation. The *Chronicle* itself reads 1134. The month and day, however, are clearly indicted. Adam's use of March 20 is erroneous. The *Chronicle* on the two pages cited in the beginning of this note states that March 25 is the date of foundation, while March 20 is the day on which the abbot and monks were selected for the new foundation. Finally, Dechanet's dates (see *William* p. 43) are also drawn from Janauschek, *op. cit.* p. 34. However, Déchanet is wrong when he states that March 21, 1134 was the date on which the decision to found the monastery was made. The *Chronicle* clearly reads that this was March 20, 1134; see Delisle, *op. cit.*, pp. 645-646.

38. Poncelet, *op. cit.*, p. 90.

39. The desire to become a Cistercian had been felt by William at least as early as his first visit to Bernard, for he tells us in the *Vita prima Bernardi* that when he met Bernard he was filled with a desire to remain with him and share his life; see PL 185:246D.

40. See Bernard's Letter 86, PL 182:210. tr. B. S. James, *The Letters of St Bernard of Clairvaux* (London: Burns Oates, 1953) Letter 88, pp. 127-128.

41. See Ceglar, *op. cit.*, pp. 167-192 for a discussion of the date of William's arrival at Signy as September, 1135.

42. Charles LeCouteulx, *Annales ordinis cartusiensis* (Montreuil-sur-Mer, 1887) Vol. 2, p. 91 indicates that both the obituaries of Signy and of the Carthusian house of Mont Dieu furnish September 8. The year depends on a document in the archives of Mont Dieu which says that William died "about the time of the Council of Reims held under Pope Eugene"; see LeCouteulx, *op. cit.*, p. 90. The council was held in March, 1148. Both Vacandard (*op. cit.*, Vol. 1, p. xx) and Adam (*op. cit.*, pp. 98-99) are unable to determine whether 1147 or 1148 is the year of William's death. Dechanet, however, definitely takes 1148 without giving any evidence to substantiate this alternative; see his *William* p. 109 n. 187.

by an illness which left him broken and unable to share fully in the rigors of the life there.[43] Unable to share in the manual labor, William gave himself to writing.[44] His written works have been enumerated and examined by various authors and need not be treated here.[45] It remains only to add that some martyrologies mention William not on September 8, but on January 12.[46] This latter date is probably[47] the date on which William's body was moved from its resting place in the cloister at Signy[48] to a wall in the church there.[49]

43. Poncelet, *op. cit.*, p. 92.

44. Poncelet, *op. cit.*, pp. 92-93.

45. The works of William of St Thierry have been treated by Adam and Déchanet in their monographs on William's life and works. Dom Wilmart's article "La série et la date des ouvrages de Guillaume de Saint-Thierry" cited in note 5 above is indispensable for any examination of these works.

46. William's remembrance is made on January 12 in *Acta sanctorum, Januarius,* (Antwerp, 1643) Vol. 1, p. 719; see also Adam, *op. cit.*, p. 101 n. 2 for inclusion of William on this same date in *Menologium cisterciensee* and Menard's *Martyrologium sanctorum ordinis divi Benedicti.* However, A.M. Zimmermann OSB, enters William in the section for September 8 in his *Kalendarium Benedictinum* (Vienna, 1933) Vol. 3, pp. 29-30.

47. Adam, *op. cit.*, p. 101. The translation of the body was tantamount to beatification; see Déchanet, "Guillaume de Saint-Thierry," *Dictionnaire de spiritualite* (1965) Vol. 6, col. 1243.

48. Delisle, *op. cit.*, p. 649.

49. The *Chronicle of Signy* indicates that the reburial of William's body took place during the second term of Abbot Giles; see Delisle, *op. cit.*, pp. 653-654. Giles is identified as the tenth and the thirteenth abbot of Signy; he served two terms with an interval in between. The story of his first abbacy is told; see Delisle, *op. cit.*, p. 653. Adam, *op. cit.*, p. 99, deals with this material very well. Although he assigns a definite date of January 12, he assigns no year to the reburial; see Adam, *op. cit.*, p. 101 n. 1. Déchanet, on the other had, is guilty of a slip of the pen when he deals with this same material. He says in *William* p. 110 that on January 12, 1215, Giles II, ninth Abbot of Signy, had the bones of William reburied. Since Déchanet cites Adam and the *Chronicle of Signy* as his only sources, one can only assume that Déchanet has taken *Egidius . . . secundo factus est abbas Signiaci et prefuit eidem ecclesie ix annis* to mean that Giles II was ninth Abbot of Signy! The correct reading, of course, is that Giles was made Abbot of Signy for a second time and was in charge of the Abbey for nine years. Déchanet's assignment of 1215 as the year for this event is highly questionable inasmuch as our chronology for the abbots of Signy lacks sufficient facts to verify this year with exactness. See *Gallia christiana,* Vol. 9, p. 305ff.

THE *ENIGMA OF FAITH,* ITS NATURE AND PURPOSE

Three medieval lists serve to identify the works which make up the literary corpus of William of St Thierry.[1] The first is provided by William himself. It is contained in a letter sent to Haymo, prior of Mont Dieu.[2] This letter serves as an introduction to the letter to the Carthusians of Mont Dieu, *The Golden Epistle.* A second listing is provided by the *Vita antiqua.*[3] The third list is found on the first folio of the *Liber legendarum sancti Theodorici* in a fifteenth-century manuscript of unknown origin, which is now in the municipal library at Reims.[4] In all three of these lists the *Enigma of Faith* is mentioned with its companion treatise the *Mirror of Faith.* The Reims manuscript simply lists these two treatises among the other works by William.[5] The *Vita antiqua* does little more than this. It states briefly:

> He composed two little books and of these he called one the *Enigma of Faith* and the other the *Mirror of Faith*; in these he showed succinctly and clearly what was to be believed.[6]

The Letter to Haymo has more to say about the *Mirror* and the *Enigma.* It informs us that the one treatise is entitled the *Mirror* because it is simple and straightforward, while the other is called the *Enigma* because it is somewhat more involved.[7] In addition, William indicates a similarity between the *Enigma* and his no-longer-extant *Sentences on the Faith.*[8]

1. Adam, *op. cit.,* pp. 8-11.
2. William of St Thierry, *The Golden Epistle,* CF 12 (Spencer, 1971) pp. 3-8.
3. Poncelet, *op. cit.*
4. This text is available in Adam, *op. cit.,* p. 11; see also, Wilmart, "La série et la date" for a discussion of William's works and their chronology.
5. Adam, *op. cit.,* p. 11.
6. Poncelet, *op. cit.,* p. 93.
7. William of St Thierry, *The Golden Epistle,* CF 12, p. 5.
8. William of St Thierry, *The Golden Epistle,* CF 12, p. 7. In 1911 Martin Grabmann stated that he found the lost *Sentences* in the Bibliothèque Nationale; see *Die Geschichte der scholastichen Methode* (Freiburg, 1911) Vol. 2, 109-110. Dom Wilmart criticised Grabmann's opinion on this matter, and rejected it, in "Un conjecture mal fondée au sujet des Sentences de Guillaume de Saint-Thierry," *Revue bénédictine* 35 (1923) pp. 263-267.

In this letter William tells his reason for writing the *Mirror* and the *Enigma*: some of the monks at Signy had requested them from him as a support to their faith and as a source of consolation. William had written these treatises for his confreres at Signy some years before, but now at a later date wished to dedicate them to the Carthusians at Mont Dieu,[9] for whom he had a great affection resulting, at least in part, from his visit to their house around 1144.[10] His love for the monks at Mont Dieu and for their life of solitude prompted him to dedicate the *Mirror* and the *Enigma* to them, as a document from the archives of Mont Dieu relates.[11] In view of the dedication to the monks at Mont Dieu it would seem reasonable to suppose that copies of the two treatises on faith were sent to the Carthusians along with *The Golden Epistle*. However, there is no evidence to support this supposition. Charleville MS 114, which belonged to the Abbey of Signy, is the only extant twelfth-century manuscript of these two treatises.

While the addressees and the purpose of these two works on faith are known, their date of composition is not. William mentions them in his Letter to Haymo, second prior of Mont Dieu, who was in office from 1144-1150.[12] Therefore William could have sent this letter anytime from 1144 to the time of his own death in 1147 or 1148. It is generally agreed that the treatises were written after Abelard's condemnation at Sens in 1140.[13] Thus, the two works can be dated during the last seven or eight years of William's life.

The exact relationship between the two treatises and Peter Abelard is not made clear by William. As Adam has already stated, William does not indicate any relationship between

---

9. William of St Thierry, *The Golden Epistle*, CF 12, p. 4, n. 9.

10. Adam gives no date for William's visit to Mont Dieu; Déchanet says the visit must have been around 1144: see his *William* p. 97. Mont Dieu is in the diocese of Reims, within a few miles of the city of Sedan; see LeCouteulx, *op. cit.*, Vol. 1, p. 404.

11. LeCouteulx, *op. cit.*, Vol. 2, pp. 90-91.

12. LeCouteulx, *op. cit.*, Vol. 2, p. 113.

13. Wilmart, "La série et la date," p. 163; Adam, *op. cit.*, p. 69; Déchanet, *William* p. 70.

these two works and his *Disputation against Abelard.*[14] In fact, William explicitly relates the *Enigma* to only one other work of his: the *Sentences on the Faith,* a work no longer extant. Recent scholarship, however, views the *Enigma* as part of William's polemic against the teachings of Abelard.[15] Odo Brooke characterized the treatise in this way:

> Unlike the works directed ex professo against Abelard and de Conches, William's aim here is not simply to answer his opponents with a refutation of their errors, but with a fully developed theology on very different lines, dominated . . . by the sense of the mystery of the Trinity.[16]

Brooke, however, never points to specific passages of the *Enigma* which show a relationship to Abelard or his teachings. D. E. Luscombe accepts Brooke's position on the *Enigma* and states that William must be seen not simply as an informer against Abelard, but as a powerful thinker who attempted to meet Abelard on a speculative level in this work.[17] Luscombe makes this statement in passing; he does not profess to have studied the *Enigma of Faith,* nor does he provide any textual evidence to prove his point. Furthermore, Davy, who edited the *Enigma* and translated it, does not furnish any evidence in her introduction or her notes that might allow the treatise to be classified as part of the anti-Abelardian polemic of the twelfth century. Thus no scholar has done more than make general assertions that the *Enigma* is a treatise written against Peter Abelard. And William himself says nothing to indicate any relation between what he says in the *Enigma* and the teachings of Abelard. Much work

14. Adam, *op. cit.,* pp. 69-70.

15. See Déchanet, "Guillaume de Saint-Thierry," *Dictionnaire de spiritualité,* Vol. 6 (1965) col. 1243. In a more recent statement Déchanet has shifted his position to a more inclusive, general, view of the causes prompting the request of the monks of Signy that William write the *Enigma.* In the Introduction to Mother Columba Hart's translation, *William of St Thierry: Exposition on the Song of Songs,* CF 6 (Spencer, 1970) p. xi, n. 18, Déchanet says the monks at Signy were troubled by the innovations of Abelard and *others.*

16. Brooke, "The Speculative Development of the Trinitarian Theology of William of St Thierry in the *Aenigma fidei,*" RTAM 27 (1960) p. 194.

17. Luscombe, *The School of Peter Abelard* (Cambridge, 1969) p. 111.

remains to define clearly the precise relationship between the *Enigma* and Abelard. An indispensable part of such an attempt must involve the study of the text of the *Enigma* and the texts of Abelard.

While the *Enigma* deals with some of the same areas of theological investigation which prompted William's initial concern over Abelard — faith and the Trinity — it is essentially a constructive attempt to grapple with the problem of man and his knowledge of God with the focus on the Divine Names. There are no allusions to the exposition, condemnation, and correction of Abelard's errors found in William's *Disputation*. Furthermore, the intensely polemical tone of that treatise is lacking in the *Enigma*.[18] In this work William does not appear to address himself to the errors of Peter Abelard which had prompted his letter to Bernard of Clairvaux in 1138. This is evident, for example, in the fact that William, who previously expressed shock at Abelard's use of *aestimatio* to define faith as *aestimatio rerum non apparentium*[19] does not hesitate in the *Enigma* to use this same word in a somewhat analogous way.[20] This is not to assert that William defined faith as he accused Abelard of having done; rather, it indicates that William is not writing with Abelard in mind, at least not to the degree that was true of the *Disputation*. William is not using language in a tight polemical manner against Abelard as he had done in the *Disputation*.

William had also criticized Abelard in Chapter Six of the *Disputation* for his rejection of *gratia adjuvans*, God's continuing enabling grace.[21] However, while the *Enigma* reveals William's characteristic view of the importance of grace,[22] it nowhere alludes to *gratia adjuvans*. Thus, in this treatise

18. Brooke, *op. cit.*, p. 205, holds that there is an underlying polemical motif in the *Enigma*.

19. *Disputatio*, PL 180:249A. See Luscombe, *op. cit.*, p. 112, for a discussion of Abelard's definition of faith.

20. See Par. 58 of the *Enigma*, below.

21. PL 180:266-269; see Luscombe, *op. cit.*, pp. 129-130, for a discussion of Abelard's and William's positions.

22. William's view of the importance of grace is especially evident in his Exp Rm.

William does not appear to be concerned primarily with the
teachings of Peter Abelard. The extent to which Abelard's
influence is felt in the *Enigma* however, will be indicated
below.[23]

The *Enigma of Faith* can best be understood as a treatise
written by a monk for monks at a particular monastery. The
avowed purpose in William's writing it, as mentioned above,
was to provide consolation to the monks at Signy and to
bolster their faith.[24] The specific problems which prompted
the monks to request such assistance are nowhere explicitly
set forth. Odo Brooke is near the mark when he states that
the *Enigma* represents William's reply to contemporary ratio-
nalistic tendencies in theology as seen in the teachings of men
like Abelard, William of Conches, and Gilbert of Porrée.[25] It
is known that some of Abelard's works were at Signy while
William was a monk there.[26] It was William's reading of these
works that initiated his entrance into the controversy con-

23. See below in this section, pp. 15-16.

24. When William refers to the *Mirror* and the *Enigma* in his letter to Haymo, he
says he was urged by his fellow monks to write the two treatises because of their
need for assistance to bolster their faith. William calls their situation more anxious
than dangerous. There is no indication in his words of an immediate threat to the
faith of the monks. This appears to be evidence that the *Enigma* cannot be
considered a polemical treatise ex professo.

25. Brooke, *op. cit.,* p. 196.

26. In this letter William claims to have read a work which he calls *Theologia
Petri Abaelardi* (PL 182:531C). This work, William says, consisted of two *libelli,*
both of which dealt with almost the same topics (PL 182:531D). There is some
disagreement among scholars about which of Abelard's works are meant here.
Adam, *op. cit.,* p. 63, and Déchanet, *William* p. 55, have stated that the works
meant are the *Theologia christiana* and the *Introductio ad theologiam;* the latter
work is also called the *Theologia Scholarium.* This choice seems very likely, since
these two treatises are the result of Abelard's revision of the *Theologia Summi
boni* which had been condemned and burnt at Soissons in 1121; see Luscombe,
op. cit., pp. 104 and 105. However, Luscombe, *op. cit.,* p. 106, contends that the
two *libelli* were the *Theologia Scholarium* and the *Liber sententiarum;* Abelard
denied that the second of these works was his; see PL 178:107D. The *Liber,* by
the way, is no longer extant. The entire matter is further complicated by the fact
that in his Adv Abl 7, PL 180:270AD, William quotes two passages from
Abelard's *Commentaria in ep. ad rom.* 2, CC Continuatio Medievalis, Vol. 11, p.
116, lines 202-209, 210-214; this, despite the fact that William does not state that
he even knew the work by Abelard. It is known, however that Bernard of
Clairvaux knew this work; thus, he may be William's source of knowledge of this
work of Abelard; see PL 182:1062D.

cerning Abelard; in 1138 he sent the *Disputation against Abelard* to Bernard of Clairvaux and Geoffrey of Chartres.[27] Furthermore, it is known that an entering novice brought William of Conches' *Summa of Philosophy* to Signy.[28] William read this work and wrote a criticism of some of its contents in his *On the Errors of William of Conches*[29] which he sent to St Bernard around 1140.[30]

The *Enigma* is a treatise quite different from the *Disputation* or the *On the Errors*, works in which William wrote against specific theologians and their erroneous teachings in a polemical manner. In the *Disputation* William speaks of Abelard as "our theologian"[31] and "Master Peter";[32] he brands Abelard's teachings as innovations: "the new theology of a new theologian."[33] In the *On the Errors* William says that William of Conches announces a new philosophy;[34] he calls his teachings vain novelties.[35] William disparages this new philosopher by alluding to some verses in Horace's *The Art of Poetry*.[36] On the contrary, however, in the *Enigma* no contemporary figure is named. There are no expressions such as "our theologian," and no caustic remarks about contemporary theologians or their teachings. Furthermore, the tone of the *Enigma* is not one of urgency. In 1138 when William

27. Déchanet, *William* p. 57. R. Klibansky contends that the Adv Abl was sent to Bernard in Lent of 1139. See his "Peter Abailard and Bernard of Clairvaux" *Medieval and Renaissance Studies* 5 (1961) p. 12, n. 1.

28. PL 180:333B.

29. PL 180:333-340.

30. There is general agreement on this date; see Adam,*op. cit.,* p. 70; Déchanet, *William* p. 64 n. 73; Wilmart, "La série et la date" p. 160 n. 1.

31. PL 180:260C.

32. PL 180:276A.

33. PL 180:255C.

34. PL 180:333A.

35. *Ibid.*

36. Speaking of the *Summa philosophiae* of William of Conches William uses the expression *magni promissor hiatus* (PL 180:333B); this is borrowed from *The Art of Poetry* 138 and is meant as an allusion to Horace's:

quid dignum tanto feret hic promissor hiatu?

parturient montes, nascetur ridiculus mus.

These lines might be translated:

Will this braggart produce anything worthwhile?

Mountains are in labor, but bring forth a mouse.

wrote to Bernard about what he felt to be a widespread and serious danger he said that he was writing about a situation of grave danger for all.[37] In his Letter to Haymo, William does not give evidence of such a feeling of immediacy. He describes the monks of Signy as "troubled by anxiety rather than threatened by danger."[38]

The *Enigma*, as Odo Brooke described it, is an assertion of tradition in reaction against unorthodox doctrine; the treatise is an attempt to evolve a theological doctrine of the relationship of faith and reason — *ratio fidei* — and to establish the author's own method of applying this doctrine.[39] As William develops his understanding of this concept of *ratio fidei*[40] he applies it to the Mystery of the Trinity. By means of a speculative trinitarian theology approached from principles opposite to those which he attributed to his opponents, William reached a very different conclusion: a rejection of the purely philosophical speculations of human reason, and an emphasis on mystery.[41]

An area where the *Enigma* can be specifically linked to two of Williams's contemporaries is that of the Divine Names, the attribution of certain names to the persons of the Trinity. This can be demonstrated from William's *On the Errors of William of Conches*. The issue of the Divine Names forms the core of William's difficulties with the teachings of William of Conches. To illustrate his objections to this theologian's position William quoted from the latter's *Summa of Philosophy*:

In the Divinity, therefore, there is power, wisdom, and will. The saints call these three persons, transferring to them because of a certain affinity, words which everyone knows, calling power Father, wisdom Son, and will the Holy Spirit. Power is called Father because he created everything and rules with paternal affection. Wisdom is called Son because

37. PL 182:531A.
38. William of St Thierry, *The Golden Epistle*, CF 12, p. 4. See note 24 above.
39. Brooke, *op. cit.*, p. 202.
40. See the section of this introduction on the sources of the *Enigma* for a discussion of *ratio fidei*.
41. Brooke, *op. cit.*, pp. 204-5.

he was begotten before the ages; because just as a son is temporally from a father, so wisdom is coeternally and consubstantially from power. In addition, divine will is called the Spirit, for spirit is properly breath . . . because in the spirit or breath often the will of a man is detected: indeed, sometimes a man breathes happily, sometimes angrily.[42]

William of St Thierry saw this position as a threat to the unity of the Trinity. He responded to this threat with several passages from Augustine and one from pseudo-Jerome; nine of these same passages occur in the *Enigma*.[43]

It is also in his work on William of Conches' teachings that William provides a connection between Abelard and the *Enigma*, for he equates the position of Abelard and William of Conches vis-a-vis the Divine Names.[44] Moreover, in the second chapter of the *Disputation against Abelard* William criticized that theologian's attribution of *potentia, sapientia*, and *charitas* or *benignitas* to the Father, Son, and Holy Spirit respectively.[45] William found fault with Abelard's manner of applying these names to the Trinity. For example, Abelard said of the names:

> just as other names are spoken about God improperly, nevertheless they are fittingly put forth as a description of him for the commendation of the Highest Good.[46]

William attacks this and says:

> And because of this we say that, since the Divinity is preached by the Catholic Fathers in the name of the Father and of the Son and of the Holy Spirit; this is a profession of faith, not a description of the Divinity, for if it could be described, it could also be circumscribed.[47]

Clearly, William of Conches and Peter Abelard are integral parts of the intellectual environment which called forth the

42. PL 180:333C.
43. For a list of these passages see the second footnote to Par. 49, below.
44. PL 180:334C.
45. PL 180:250AB.
46. Adv Abl 2, PL 180:250B.
47. Adv Abl 2, PL 180:251C.

Enigma of Faith. The teachings of these two men are essential to an understanding of the motivation which prompted William to call upon the wisdom of the Latin Fathers in an attempt to deal with the problems of faith and reason, man's knowledge of God in this life, and the attributes of God. In brief, the *Enigma* is an attempt to develop a theological methodology which can grapple with the Mystery of the Trinity without exceeding the limitations imposed upon human reason by the finite nature of man and the infinite nature of God.

SOURCES OF THE *ENIGMA OF FAITH*

A comprehensive study of the sources used by William of St Thierry has yet to be undertaken. The work which has been done in this area has been dominated by an idea which has dictated the direction of research in Williams's sources. This idea is that William used Greek sources. An early opinion on this stated that William knew Greek and made extensive use of Greek authors in his work.[1] At present, it is generally held that William knew no Greek, or at least no more than any other writer of his day.[2] That is, William knew some stock words and phrases, which were part of the learned vocabulary of the twelfth century. Most scholars today feel that William borrowed material from Greek authors through the medium of Latin translations. This is not to be denied; however, the extent to which William uses the Greek Fathers must be, it seems to me, reappraised. Little evidence has been provided to substantiate the great use of the Greeks attributed to William in almost every monograph and article dealing with him. Almost by implication William is presented as an expert Greek scholar and master of Greek theological

1. Adam, *op. cit.*, pp. 103-104.
2. For a good treatment of the knowledge of Greek in the Middle Ages see M.L. Laistner, *Thought and Letters in Western Europe* (Ithaca, 1966) pp. 238-250. Although Laistner is dealing with a slightly earlier period than the twelfth century he gives a good idea of the state of Greek studies in the early medieval period and the practice of drawing on earlier Latin authors for allusions to Greek works.

thought.[3] William himself acknowledges one source from the East: Origen.[4] This dearth of explicit acknowledgment of Greek sources is explained away by William's prudence or his originality.[6] Either explanation seems incomplete, to say the least. The study of William's sources might progress considerably if a moratorium were declared on searching for these sources among the Greeks and greater effort were exerted on the Latin masters of Western thought: Augustine, Boethius, and others.

The penchant for seeing Greek sources behind much of what William says is characteristic of comments made about the *Enigma of Faith* and its sources.[6] Déchanet says the opening lines of the *Enigma* are drawn from Origen's *Commentary on the Epistle to the Romans*.[7] In actual fact William has taken these lines from Hilary of Poitiers.[8] Likewise, Déchanet suggests an affinity between Basil the Great and William's definition of *persona*: *cujus pro sui forma,*

---

3. Déchanet, *William, passim* and esp. pp. 140-151. Also, Louis Bouyer, *The Cistercian Heritage* (London; Westminster, Md., 1958) pp. 110-124.

4. Déchanet, *Guillaume de Saint-Thierry, Exposé sur le Cantique des Cantiques,* SCh 82, (Paris, 1962) p. 32 n. 1. William's use of Origen is, of course, through the translations of Rufinus.

5. Déchanet, *Aux sources de la spiritualité de Guillaume de Saint-Thierry* (Bruges, 1940) p. 75, esp. n. 3; J. Hourlier in the Introduction to *On Contemplating God,* CF 3 (Spencer, 1971) p. 31. Déchanet says William did not openly mention his Greek sources because the times were hostile to such authors. Hourlier, speaking of William's use of Dionysian sources, calls his avoiding of Dionysius' vocabulary an example of William's "deep-seated originality." This statement does not hold when compared with what we know of William's use of his sources. He usually borrows wholesale and verbatim.

6. See Bouyer, *op. cit.,* pp. 110-124, for a discussion of the *Enigma* which typifies this tendency. For example, note: "It is obvious that William has once: again drawn on the sources of the Greek Fathers, of which his whole treatise is a veritable epitome . . . " (p. 114); also, "Here again we detect the direct influence of Origen, but given precision and balance by St. Athanasius and the Cappadocians," (p. 116).

In addition, see the two articles by O. Brooke, "The Speculative Development" pp. 208-211; "The Trinitarian Aspect of the Ascent of the Soul to God in the Theology of William of St. Thierry." RTAM 26 (1959) p. 86, n. 6; p. 120 and 124.

7. Déchanet, *William* p. 77, n. 105.

8. See the note on the opening lines of the *Enigma* below.

certa sit agnitio.[9] Actually this definition is taken from Boethius.[10] The article in the *Dictionnaire de spiritualité* on Dionysius the Pseudo-Areopagite and his influence on the Cistercians offers further examples of an attempt to see Greek authors as William's sources.[11] The author of this article says that William, especially in the *Enigma*, is clearly influenced by the Greek Fathers.[12] Fracheboud cites *supereminens, supersapere,* and *supercoelestis* from the *Enigma* and from other works by William as sure signs of the influence of Pseudo-Dionysius. However, all three of these words occur in patristic writings which antedate Pseudo-Dionysius. The first, *supereminens,* is a Pauline word; it occurs in Eph 1:19 and 3:19. Also, it is used by Hilary, Ambrose, and Augustine.[13] *Supersapere* is borrowed from Hilary by William for use in the *Enigma.*[14] *Supercoelestis* is used by Tertullian, Augustine, Jerome, and Leo the Great.[15]

At the present time there is no proof that William used any Greek sources for the *Enigma.* When he uses Greek material it is through a Latin translation or it is borrowed from some other Latin writer. For example, in the *Enigma* when William uses a definition of *Deus* from ϑεος he is borrowing from Isidore of Seville.[16] Additional examples of this use of Greek material through a Latin medium occur in William's *Exposition on the Epistle to the Romans* 2:3 which is virtually a verbatim borrowing from Augustine's *On the Spirit and the Letter* 11:18:

William, PL 180:579D	Augustine, CSEL 60:170
quae cognitio pium facit, quia pietas est vera sapientia. Pietatem dico quam Graeci	Quae cogitatio pium facit, quia pietas est vera sapientia; pietatem dico quam Graeci ϑέοσεβεια vocant;

9. Déchanet, *William* p. 83, n. 117; see Par. 34, below.
10. See the beginning of Par. 34 and footnote.
11. M.-André Fracheboud, "Les cisterciens," *Dict. de spirit.* Vol. 3 (Paris, 1957) pp. 329-340.
12. Fracheboud, *op. cit.,* p. 337.
13. Albert Blaise, *Dictionnaire latin-francais des auteurs chrétiens* (Strasbourg, 1954) p. 795.
14. See Par. 1 where *supersapere* is translated "to be excessively wise."
15. Blaise, *op. cit.,* p. 797.
16. See the first note for Par. 72.

ϑεοσέβεια vocant. Ipsa quippe commendata est in libro Job cum dicitur, "Ecce pietas est sapientia." ϑεοσέβεια enim Dei cultus est.

ipsa quippe commendata est, cum dictum est homini, quod in libro Job legitur: ecce pietas est sapientia. ϑεοσέβεια porro, si ad verbi originem latine expressam interpretaretur, dei cultus dici poterat.

Furthermore, when William refers to Greek sources he has a translation in mind. In his *Exposition on Romans* his comments on Rom 1:4, *qui praedestinatus est Filius Dei*, are borrowed from Rufinus' translation of Origen's *Commentary on the Epistle to the Romans* 1:5:

William, PL 180:550C
secundum graecae translationis veritatem, non praedestinatus, sed destinatus est.

Origen, PG 14:849A
Quamvis enim in Latinis exemplaribus praedestinatus soleat inveniri, tamen secundum quod interpretationis veritas habet destinatus scriptum est, non praedestinatus.

Another example of William's apparent use of a Greek source is found in this same work where he comments on Rom 12:3, *Non plus sapere, quam oportet sapere, sed sapere ad sobrietatem.* William again is borrowing from Rufinus' translation of Origen:

William, PL 180:672B
Graecus non sobrietatem hic habet, sed temperatiam σωφρονεῖν (sic).

Origen, PG 14:1210C
quod in Graeco decitur σωφροσύνη in nostris autem codicibus, hoc est in Scripturis divinis, sobrietas a mejoribus interpretatum est, ab aliis tamen eruditis viris[17] temperantia ponitur.

The sources actually used by William for the *Enigma of Faith* are, in his own words, the Scriptures and the Fathers.[18]

17. The *eruditi viri* referred to in this text include Augustine who sometimes uses the reading *sed sapere ad temperantiam* for Rom 12:3. See *Tractatus in Johannis evangelium* 74:3 and *Ad Orosium contra Priscillianistas et Origenistas* 11:14.

18. See Par. 71. Furthermore, William describes the sources of the *Enigma* in his Letter to Haymo as "the words and the thought of the Catholic Fathers" (CF 12, p. 5).

William makes abundant use of the Vulgate Bible. However, there is only occasional use of the historical books of the Old Testament, and then only Genesis, Exodus, and Deuteronomy. The wisdom literature is used: Job, Psalms, Proverbs, Ecclesiastes, Wisdom, and Ecclesiasticus. Of these only the Psalms are employed with any frequency. The prophets are used sparingly, Isaiah most frequently. Of the New Testament books William uses all of the Gospels, especially that of John. There are only a few borrowings from Acts. Most of the Pauline letters are used, with the exception of 1 Thessalonians, Titus, and Philemon. Extensive use is made of Romans, 1 Corinthians, and 2 Corinthians. Of the Catholic Epistles only 1 John is used. Finally, there are a few references to the Apocalypse.

For non-biblical sources William drew from a small number of authors: Hilary, Augustin, pseudo-Jerome (Pelagius), Leo the Great, Boethius, and Isidore of Seville. William's use of Hilary's *Trinity* and his *Tracts on the Psalms* has been undetected until now. The primary source for the *Enigma* is without a doubt Augustine's *Trinity*. Of the fifteen books of this work William quotes passages verbatim from nine. In addition to the *Trinity* William drew from *On Genesis (De genesi ad litteram), Tracts on John, On True Religions, On Christian Doctrine, Letters* 92, 120, 147, and 170. Also, there is a possible use of the *City of God, On the Merits and Forgiveness of Sins, Against Julian* and the *Enarrations on the Psalms*. Of the other authors William uses only one or two works: Leo, *Sermons* 76 and 77; Boethius, *On Person and Two Natures* and the *Trinity*; Isidore, *Etymologies*. Of these authors all but one are known to have been represented in the library at Signy[19] The exception is Isidore, the first half of whose *Etymologies* is known to have been at the Benedictine monastery of St Thierry during the twelfth

19. Déchanet, *Guillaume de Saint-Thierry, Exposé sur le Cantique des Cantiques,* SCh 82, p. 54 n. 2 and his *William* p. 48 n. 10 and p. 68 n. 79. Déchanet does not provide a complete or detailed catalogue of the Signy manuscripts in the Charleville library. It has, therefore, been impossible to determine with any precision the Signy holdings.

century.[20] It is from this first half of Isidore's work that William drew his definition of *Deus*.

In addition to these sources there are also allusions to, or borrowings from, William's own works; for example, *Exposition on the Epistle to the Romans, On Contemplating God, On the Nature and Dignity of Love,* and *On the Errors of William of Conches.*

Two additional aspects of the problem of William's sources remain to be considered. These are the Divine Names and William's use of *ratio fidei.* The presence of the expression *nomina divina* in the treatise has led some scholars to declare rather hastily that William used the *On the Divine Names* of Pseudo-Dionysius.[21] This seems improbable; an examination of the translation of the treatise *On the Divine Names* by John Scotus Erigena[22] gives no indication that William used that work as a source for his *Enigma.* While he may be ultimately indebted to Pseudo-Dinonysius for the expression *nomina divina* William's concepts, terminology, and divisions of the Divine Names are essentially Augustinian. Augustine does not use the expression *nomina divine* in his *Trinity,* but he is the source for William's treatment of the names. William deals with the Divine Names by means of these categories: *secundum substantiam, secundum accidens,* and *ad aliquid.* He says:

> Numquam enim de Deo dicitur aliquid secundum accidens, sed neque semper secundum substantiam. Dicitur enim et ad aliquid.[23]

This has been borrowed from Augustine's *Trinity*:

> In deo autem nihil quidem secundum accidens dicitur quia nihil in eo mutabile est; nec tamen omne quod dicitur secundum substantiam dicitur. Dicitur enim ad aliquid sicut pater ad filium et filius ad patrem.[24]

20. See the first volume of W. M. Lindsay, *Isidori hispalensis episcopi etymologiarum sive originum libri xx* (Oxford, 1911) p. viii.
21. See for example Fracheboud, *op. cit.,* pp. 335-337.
22. *De divinis nominibus,* PL 122:1111-1172.
23. See Par. 43.
24. *De trin.* 5:5.

William also speaks of names used *ad se* or *substantialiter* but these again are Augustinian categories.[25] In William's general attitude toward the Divine Names, as well as in his terminology, he is indebted to Augustine.

William nowhere uses the terminology of Pseudo-Dionysius as translated by Erigena. The many compounds with the prefix *super* are, perhaps, the most characteristic feature of Dionysian expression in the treatise on the Divine Names: *superessentialis, superdeus, superbonus, supereminenter, superplenitudo, superoptimus, supersapiens, superexcellens, superexaltatus, superexistens, superprincipalis*. These are some of the characteristic compounds which occur throughout the Dionysian treatise. None of them occurs in William's *Enigma*. In addition, William's terms *essentiale nomen* and *relative nomen* are not to be found in *On the Divine Names*.

The final aspect of the problem of William's sources to be considered in his use of *ratio fidei*. In the *Enigma of Faith* William fully develops and uses the concept of *ratio fidei*. The expression occurs no less than twenty-two times in the treatise. *Ratio fidei* is an expression of a reconciliation of the tension between faith and reason.[26] This phrase expresses a view of faith and reason which subordinates reason to faith, but not in an anti-intellectual, or repressive, way. Reason is not rejected; no hint is given of "blind faith." What is meant is a *ratio* which investigates and scrutinizes the content of *fides* but with certain limitations which are imposed by the very nature of the content of that faith: mystery. William says on this point:

> However, this way of speaking about God has its own discipline supported by the rules and limits of faith so as to teach a manner of speaking about God reasonably according to the reasoning of faith and to prepare men to think about and perceive the ineffable in an ineffable way.[27]

---

25. See the second note for Par. 46.
26. As Déchanet has indicated, the phrase is equivalent to the more recent theological term: *ratio theologica*. See his *William* p. 79.
27. See Par. 41.

This *ratio*, as William says in the *Mirror of Faith,* is not *ratio* as used by man in any other human situation. "The reasoning of faith is at odds with ordinary human reason."[28] *Ratio fidei* is informed by faith; faith provides its shape, methodology, and content. Faith, says William, shapes a reasoning for itself which is *sui generis.*[29] *Ratio fidei* provides a way of thinking and speaking about God that possesses its own concepts and terminology intelligible only when viewed from the vantage point of faith:

> this manner of speaking about God has certain special words which are rational but not intelligible except in the reasoning of faith, not however in the reasoning of human understanding.[30]

William's contribution with reference to *ratio fidei* is his full and mature use of this concept in the *Enigma.* The expression itself is as old as the Latin translations of St Paul where *ratio fidei* occurs in Rom 12:6:

> Habentes autem donationes secundum gratiam, quae data est nobis, differentes: sive prophetiam secundum rationem fidei. . .

In this verse, however, *secundum rationem fidei* was generally interpreted by the Fathers as *secundum mensuram fidei.*[31] In fact, there are some instances where the latter expression is used to translate the Greek original of this verse.[32] There are, however, examples of the use of *ratio fidei* independent of Rom 12:6 which are similar to William's use of the phrase. These occur in Hilary of Poitiers,[33] Gregory the Great,[34]

---

28. Davy, *Deux traités sur la foi* p. 38.
29. See Par. 41.
30. See Par. 41.
31. For example, Jerome, *Commentarius in ep. ad rom.* 12, comments on Rom 12:6 with "Each receives in proportion to his belief." The phrase in Rom 12:6 cited by Jerome is *secundum rationem fidei.*
32. Jerome, *Adversus Jovinianum* 2:22 and Rufinus' translation of Origen's *Commentarius in ep. ad rom.* 9:3.
33. Hilary, *De trinitate* 1:22.
34. Gregory, *Moralia in Job* 1:28.

Anselm of Canterbury,[35] and Bernard of Clairvaux,[36] In these authors, as well as in the works of William himself, exclusive of the *Enigma of Faith*,[37] *ratio fidei* occurs randomly without systematic use and development. It is only in the *Enigma* that the concept of *ratio fidei* comes into its own and becomes the predominant expression of a reconciliation of faith and reason which respects the integrity of the mysteries of faith. This is, perhaps, William's major contribution in the *Enigma* to the development of a speculative theology.[38] William is not primarily a speculative theologian; rather, he is a mystical theologian, central to the development of the spirituality of the Cistercians Order.[39] This spirituality centered on a concern for the unfolding of God's plan of salvation in the individual soul.[40]

SUMMARY OF *MIRROR OF FAITH* AND *ENIGMA OF FAITH*

The *Mirror of Faith* and the *Enigma of Faith* are two halves of a single work. Their unity can be expressed by the verse of St Paul from which they draw their titles:

35. Anselm, *Cur Deus Homo* 1:3.

36. Bernard, *Sermones super Cantica* 20:5; ed. Leclercq, et al., *Sancti Bernardi Opera*, I (Rome, 1957)120; tr. E. Mullaney, CF 1:154.

37. See *Spec fid* 16:9-10 in Davy, *Deux traités sur la foi* p. 38; *Er Guil*, PL 180:334C; Adv Abl, PL 180:252C, 261B; *Exp Rm* 7, PL 180:673BC. In the last work William uses Rufinus' translation of Origen's *Comm. in ep. ad rom.* 9:3 where there is a discussion of the translation of the Greek version of Rom 12:6 with the Latin phrase *secundum rationem fidei*; this Latin translation is criticized as inadequate. William rejects the suggested improvement, *secundum analogiam*, and explicates it with *id est, rectam fidei regulam*. This text provides evidence of William's understanding of Rom 12:6 and reveals this verse as a primary source for his use of *ratio fidei*. An essential text for William's understanding of this verse is Augustine's *De doctrina christiana* 4:20 where the verse occurs with the phrase *sive prophetiam secundum regulam fidei*. It is known that William was familiar with this work of Augustine from his use of it in the *Enigma*. It now becomes clearer that there is a connection between William's *ratio fidei* and Augustine's *regula fidei* as used throughout the *De trin*. Apropos to this discussion is William's use in the *Enigma* of a sentence from the *De trin*. 15:28 which contains the phrase *regula fidei*; see Par. 23.

38. See Brooke, "The Speculative Development," RTAM 27 (1960) pp. 193-211 and 28 (1961) pp. 26-58.

39. Hubert Jedin, ed., *Handbuch der Kirchengeschichte* 3:2 (Freiburg, 1968) p. 54.

40. Brooke, "The Trinitarian Aspect of the Ascent of the Soul," p. 86.

For now we see through a mirror in an enigma, but then face to face. Now I know in part; then I shall understand fully, even as I have been fully understood.[1]

The two treatises concern the two modes of experience mentioned in St Paul's verse: seeing and knowing. The vision of God and the knowledge of God here on earth and in heaven are the subjects of these treatises. The *Mirror* deals primarily with faith, the means of seeing and knowing God in this life. The *Enigma* concerns itself especially with the object of this vision and cognition: God, who is Father, Son, and Holy Spirit. William distinguished between the two works in this way:

That work is divided into two books, the first of which, because it is straightforward and easy, I entitled the *Mirror of Faith*: the second, because it will be found to contain a summary of the grounds and the formulations of faith according to the words and the thought of the Catholic Fathers and is a little more obscure, the *Enigma of Faith*.[2]

The nature and scope of the *Mirror* and the *Enigma* can be briefly indicated by a summary of each treatise.

In the *Mirror of Faith* William discusses the importance of faith, hope, and love for the Christian life. The three are absolutely necessary for man and are inextricably bound together as a trinity of virtues with which man must strive to attain union with the Trinity of Father, Son, and Holy Spirit. William discourses on faith as a gift of God which requires humility and submissiveness from its recipient. Likewise, love is necessary. The unbeliever lacks faith because he lacks love.

Why do you not believe, O unbeliever? Indeed, because you do not love. You do not believe because you do not love; you do not love because you do not believe. For one is impossible without the other because one depends on the other.[3]

1. 1 Cor 13:12.
2. William of St Thierry, *The Golden Epistle*, CF 12, p. 5.
3. Spec fid, Davy, *Deux traités sur la foi: Le Miroir de la foi, L'Enigme de la foi* (Paris, 1959) p. 36.

Also, throughout his discussion William stresses the necessity of grace. Grace is the mother of our spiritual birth and life. Grace gives man birth, nurses him, and nourishes him as it leads him to perfection.[4]

William condemns the error of measuring God's mysteries by the yardstick of the human understanding.[5] *Ratio fidei* is not commensurate with ordinary human reason.[6] William counsels that doubts and temptations to disbelief be cast aside by an unswerving fidelity to the authority of Scriptures and the Fathers under the guidance of the Holy Spirit. Various temptations against faith are discussed, and various degrees of faith are treated.

Continually stressing the role of the Holy Spirit, the author surveys the sacraments as aids in the Christian's journey toward God. The content of faith is treated, including the mystery of the Trinity which forms the substance of the *Enigma of Faith*. The treatise closes with passages on the Holy Spirit as the unity of the Father and the Son, on the Trinity itself, and on man and his desire for union with God the Trinity.[7]

The *Enigma of Faith*, a slightly longer treatise than the *Mirror*, can be divided into five sections of unequal length:[8]

1. Vision and knowledge of God
2. Faith in the Trinity
3. Degrees of knowledge
4. Divine Names
5. Contemplation of the Mystery of the Trinity

These headings have been employed in the translation of the *Enigma* to facilitate dealing with an otherwise somewhat unwieldy text.

4. *Ibid.*

5. Davy, *op. cit.*, p. 38.

6. *Ibid.*

7. Spec fid has been critically edited by Déchanet in *Guillaume de Saint-Thierry, Le Miroir de la foi* (Bruges, 1946) and is available in English translation: Geoffrey Webb and Adrian Walker, *The Mirror of Faith by William of St Thierry* (London, 1959).

8. For other attempts to divide the treatise into logical sections see Davy, *op. cit.*, pp. 19-20; Déchanet, *William* p. 79 n. 110; O. Brooke, "The Speculative Development," pp. 195-196.

In the first section of the *Enigma* William discusses the inability of man to penetrate the mystery of God. Still, the author says, man has an obligation to strive to see and to know God as best he can and to the degree that God allows. God can be seen in this life through faith. William discusses the nature of this vision of faith and describes how a man must cooperate with the grace of God to attain such a vision. At one point William addresses a prayer to God in which he expresses his desire to see God, laments his inability to do so, and asks God to show him the light of truth. William then surveys the human situation and God's coming to man in Christ to lead him to perfection. This section continues with a discussion of faith and the vision and knowledge of things past and future. The author ends by describing three categories of things which can be seen.

The second section of the treatise deals with the Trinity. It begins by considering the Trinity's relation to the three categories set forth at the end of the first section. Man is wedded to creation and the physical, and images of his surroundings plague his attempts to contemplate the unseen God. William laments this situation in a prayer recognizing man's need for purification. There follows almost immediately another prayer in which he expresses an aversion to the complexities of human sophistry and a preference for the simple purity of the Scriptures. He asks God's help that he may persevere in seeking him. Terms for talking about God multiplied out of necessity as heresy arose. These terms must be used properly according to the reasoning of faith (*ratio fidei*). Various terms including *persona* are mentioned and examined. William ends this section with a confession of faith in the Trinity and a description of how our knowledge of God progresses by degrees.

The third and briefest section of the treatise deals with this progression and develops the three degrees of our knowledge of God. The section closes with an admonition to proceed humbly and piously in an attempt to understand God through faith.

The fourth is the longest of the five sections of the *Enigma*.
It concerns the Divine Names. This section displays an order
and a unity independent of the rest of the treatise and is
considered a separate treatise which William joined together
with other material to form the *Enigma*[9] The summary of
this section is best dealt with in an outline of its seven parts:

1. Divine Names are basic for a knowledge of God
2. Observe with care how these names are to be construed
3. Essential names
4. Mystery of the Trinity and the unworthiness of human
   words
5. Relative names
6. Closing remarks on preceding names
7. Name of "God"

The final section of the treatise involves the contemplation of
the Mystery of the Trinity. A prayer expressing the fear and
trembling of the author precedes this investigation of the
Trinity. This is followed by an exposition of the faith concerning the Trinity and sections treating the three Persons of
the Godhead individually.

THE ENIGMA OF FAITH: MSS, EDITIONS, AND TRANSLATIONS

William of St Thierry's *Enigma of Faith* is extant in a
unique twelfth-century manuscript, Charleville 114, in the
municipal library of Charleville, France.[1] This manuscript is a
work of several scribes and thus cannot be considered an
autograph of William himself; however, one scholar feels that
it may have been written under the direct supervision of the

9. Brooke, "The Speculative Development" p. 196.
1. Déchanet, "Un recueil singulier d'opuscules de Guillaume de Saint-Thierry:
Charleville 114," *Scriptorium* 6 (1952) p. 201. The MS contains 179 parchment
leaves; the pages measure 245 x 170 mm.; the text measures 230 x 150 mm. Dom
Jean Leclercq reports a fifteenth-century MS of the *Enigma* in Uppsala in the
University Library: Universitets Biblioteket C. 79, fols. 54-96. See his "Textes et
manuscrits cisterciens en Suède," *Analecta sacri ordinis cisterciensis* 6 (1950) p.
128. This manuscript of the *Enigma* is apparently nowhere mentioned by either
Davy or Déchanet.

author.[2] Charleville 114 originated in the monastery of Signy sometime during the twelfth century; the *ex libris* of the monastery is found on the verso of the last folio of the manuscript,[3] which is the sole witness from the twelfth century for four of William's works: *Mirror of Faith, Enigma of Faith, Meditation* 13, and the *Exposition on the Song of Songs.*[4]

The *Enigma* has been printed three times.[5] The first printing was that of Bertrand Tissier in the *Bibliotheca patrum cisterciensium.*[6] The second was the Paris reprint of Tissier's edition published by Migne in 1885.[7] The latest is that of M.-M. Davy.[8] None of these three can be considered a critical edition; the publication of such an edition remains to be done. The only translation of the *Enigma* prior to that given in this volume is the French translation accompanying the Latin text of Davy, who has done much to present to the world the text of the *Enigma.* The Davy edition, published together with the *Mirror of Faith,* offers text, translation, notes, and an *index verborum.* In addition, there is a brief stylistic study of the text. The edition, however, has some inadequacies and weak points. Much of the stylistic study of the *Enigma* can be disregarded. It has the great weakness of being a study of language which is not always William's but that of his sources. The majority of Davy's examples are not the language of William, but that of Augustine. Thus, Davy's stylistic study must be examined carefully and her examples scrutinized before any value can be placed on her findings.

2. Guitton, *Catalogue général des bibliothèques publiques des départements* 5, Fourth Series (Paris, 1879) p. 601.

3. Déchanet, *op. cit.,* p. 196, n. 2.

4. Déchanet, *op. cit.,* p. 199, n. 14. Also contained in the manuscript are *The Golden Epistle* and its introductory Letter to Prior Haymo. The Uppsala MS mentioned in note one above contains the *Mirror,* the *Enigma* and the *Exposition on the Song of Songs;* see Leclercq's article, p. 128.

5. In 1942 Déchanet expressed an intention of publishing and translating the *Enigma,* but he has not yet realized this intention. See his *Guillaume de Saint-Thierry, l'homme et son oeuvre* (Bruges, 1942) p. x, n. 6.

6. Tome 4 (Bonne Fontaine, 1662) pp. 93-112.

7. PL 180:397-440.

8. *Deux traités sur la foi, Le miroir de la foi, L'Enigme de la foi* (Paris, 1959).

Orthography in the Davy text of the treatise is problematic. The Latin text is fraught with misspellings, some of which are immediately apparent, while others deceptively suggest an alternate reading of the text. Another problem centers on the manuscript spelling and Davy's treatment of it. She provides some brief guidelines for her procedure in handling the manuscript orthography.[9] However, these guidelines do not alert the reader to various alterations in spelling which she adopts in her text of the *Enigma*. The Latin text presents a uniform orthography which does not represent what is in the manuscript. This is the chief flaw in Davy's edition of the treatise.

Additional manifestations of this same failure to represent the manuscript faithfully can be found in the absence of any attempt to report marginalia, corrections, and superscripts in the manuscript. For example, a marginal addition to the text occurs on fol. 102[r] in MS 114:

> Tres autem persone etsi non possunt simul dici; non tamen nisi simul debent intelligi.

There are further corrections, additions, or other matters of note on several folios in the manuscript, none of which is reported in Davy's text. This is unfortunate and somewhat curious since there is such a dearth of manuscripts of the *Enigma* to work with. The closest Davy comes to providing textual information of this kind is a list of variants between the Migne text and the Charleville manuscript.[10]

Davy's text also contains some erroneous readings of the manuscript. In the marginal addition to the text cited above, Davy has misread an abbreviation and given the reading *enim* where the text should read *autem*. On fol 108[v] *totum* is misread for *totus*. There is one occasion in the Davy text where *Scriptura* is found in place of the correct reading, *Scripturae*.[11] This last error causes problems in the meaning of the sentence which Davy attempts to deal with in a footnote.[12]

9. Davy, *op. cit.*, p. 22.
10. Davy, *op. cit.*, pp. 183-185.
11. MS 114 fol. 96[r]
12. Davy, *op. cit.*, p. 138, n. 192 bis.

Davy's notes to the text of the *Enigma* provide some sources used by William. However, in many cases the information in the notes is incorrect or incomplete or so general as to be of little use.[13] In summary, a debt is owed to Davy for her work on William's treatise, but caution is necessary in using her edition which suffers from some major defects and many annoying minor ones.

13. Davy, *op. cit.*, p. 92, n. 1, 2, 4; p. 124, n. 155; p. 166, n. 256; p. 178, n. 300. Compare these notes of Davy with my notes below on the passages in question.

THE ENIGMA OF FAITH

THE ENIGMA OF FAITH

VISION AND KNOWLEDGE OF GOD

IT IS A CONSCIENTIOUS ADMISSION of weak human nature that it knows only this about God: God exists. Still, it is not disrespectful to investigate the essence or nature of God and the hidden decrees of his inscrutable judgment; even, indeed, to examine them closely. However, since the mind of man cannot penetrate these matters, he must admit that they are inscrutable and cannot be investigated. While some of them are proper to the religious desire of man, others are rooted in the inscrutable nature of God.[1] For this reason even the Apostle, whose faith is not grasped by a man of this world, nor his meaning explained better by the words of another than by his own,[2] was astounded in his scrutiny and examination of these matters and declared, "O the depth of the riches of the wisdom and knowledge of God; how incomprehensible are his judgments and how inscrutable his ways."[3] Therefore, where so resolute a man is afraid, religious faith in the omnipotence of God should be the measure of human reverence and our weak intellect should not presume to scrutinize something whose nature precludes close examination. When a man looks at the bright sun his power of sight is so dazzled by the brilliance of the light that, if ever curiosity induces him to search more closely for the

1. These beginning sentences are borrowed from Hilary of Poitiers' *Tractatus in psalmum* 129:1.
2. These expressions are borrowed from Hilary's *De trinitate* 9:10.
3. Rom 11:33.

35

source of the shining light, his vision is reduced to blindness; his efforts to see more result in his not seeing at all. Now if this is true, what can we expect in the things of God, who is the sun of justice? [4] Will not folly befall anyone who tries to be excessively wise? Will not the senseless languor of stupidity overwhelm the light of even a keen intellect? A lower cause does not understand the cause of a higher nature, nor does the divine plan lie within the range of human comprehension. Indeed, whatever is to be encompassed by the knowledge of a mere man must be within the reach of his weak condition. Yet, to the extent that the divine plan allows itself to be understood, we must eagerly pursue it, so that we do not lose what has been given to us through our dissatisfaction with the limitation of our gift. Is there, then, something in God which can be perceived? Indeed, there is, if you desire only that which you are capable of attaining. For the rest, if you aspire beyond that which you can attain, you will forfeit even what you could have attained.[5] To see "face to face"[6] and to understand completely is granted to no one in this life, but is promised as a reward in the next for the faith by which we now believe what we do not see. In the meantime, we have in faith the light of promised blessings. And through this faith, as if "dimly in a mirror,"[7] we gaze upon the image of future blessings and happiness.[8]

2. Now if someone asks whether God can be seen in this life by mortal man, we answer that he can, but not with the eyes of the body in the same way that we look at the sun in the sky, nor with the mind's eye, as a person sees himself seeking something or knowing something. On the contrary, God is seen in this world through faith fortified by the authority of the canonical Scriptures. However, he was seen by the Fathers, but under the appearance which he willed to

---

4. Mal 4:2.

5. This entire section from "religious faith in the omnipotence of God . . . " is borrowed from Hilary's *De trin.* 10:53.

6. Cf. 1 Cor 13:12.

7. 1 Cor 13:12.

8. The last two sentences are taken from Hilary, *Tract. in ps.* 127:11. Cf. Heb 10:1.

choose, not in his natural form.[9] For, "no one has ever seen God"[10] said the Evangelist John, in exactly the way that those things are seen which are said to be visible. Therefore, he immediately added, "The only-begotten Son who is in the bosom of the Father, he has made him known."[11] No one has ever seen God with these eyes of the body; however, the only-begotten Son who is in the bosom of the Father makes him known by an unspoken revelation, and the rational creature who is pure and holy is filled with an inexpressable vision and thus can understand the Son, inasmuch as he is the Word: not a sound striking the ears, but an image presenting itself to the mind, so that what was said by the Lord illumines a man with a clear but interior light: "Philip, who sees me, also sees the Father."[12] The desire of the truly religious man, by which he wishes to see God, does not, in my opinion, urge him to behold that form in which, when God deigns in accordance with his will, there appears that which is not God himself, but rather his desire yearns to behold him in that substance through which God is that which he is. He can be seen in this world by the pure of heart, but he cannot be comprehended.

3. But in this question of seeing God, it seems to me that there is more value in one's manner of living than in his manner of speaking. For, whoever has learned from the Lord Jesus Christ to be meek and humble of heart will make more progress in thinking about this and in praying than in reading or listening, although sometimes it is profitable both to read and to listen. However, no one should say he wants to see God if he is unwilling to expend the care worthy of so great

9. The Latin is *ea specie quam voluntas elegit, non natura formavit*. Augustine is the source for this expression: *Epistula* 147:6. All of Par. 2-3 of the *Enigma* is indebted to Augustine's treatment of the same topic in Ep 147. A comparison of the two texts in the original Latin will indicate the extent of William's dependency here. Augustine's expression is dealt with by Basilio Studer, "Ea specie videri quam voluntas elegerit, non natura formaverit," *Vetera christianorum* 6 (1969) pp. 91-143.
10. Jn 1:18.
11. Jn 1:18.
12. Jn 14:9.

an undertaking to purify his heart. No one can see God and live,[13] because it is necessary for the soul which is taken up into that unspeakable vision to be drawn out of this life. Truly, that vision belongs to another life which is greater and is promised in the world to come, but which has already begun here on earth in all the children of grace.

4. Therefore, the only-begotten Son, who silently manifests the nature and substance of the Deity to eyes which are worthy and fit for so great a vision, makes an invisible revelation even in this life. And whoever can see God invisibly, can also adhere to him invisibly.[14] For, God, "who is invisible and incorruptible and alone possesses immortality and dwells in inaccessible light, is seen by no man and can be seen by no man."[15] Because man in his body sees only bodily things, God cannot be seen by him. But if God were inaccessible to the souls of the pious, it would not be said, "Draw near to him and be enlightened."[16] And if he were invisible to the souls of the pious, it would not be said, "because we will see him as he is."[17] Let us examine this entire verse of the Epistle of John. "Beloved," he says, "now we are the children of God; it does not yet appear what we will be. But we know that when he appears we will be like him because we will see him as he is."[18] Therefore, to the extent that we will see him, we will be like him. And it is there where we see him that we shall be like him, that is, in our soul. And even now to the degree that we do not see him, we are unlike him.

5. But, who would be so very foolish as to say that we shall be like God in a bodily way? For, it is in the inner man[19] that that likeness exists by which man is renewed day by day

13. Cf. Ex 33:20.

14. Par. 4 to here is borrowed from Augustine's Ep 147. The remainder of the paragraph is taken from Augustine's Ep 92.

15. 1 Tim 6:16.

16. Ps 33:6.

17. 1 Jn 3:2.

18. *Ibid.*

19. Cf. Rom 7:22; Eph 3:16. For the patristic understanding of this expression see Augustine, *Tract. in Johannem* 86:1. The exterior man is the body; the interior man is the soul.

in the knowledge of God according to the image of him who created him.[20] And it is there that we become more like him as we progress more in knowledge and love of him. To the extent that we see him in a closer and more intimate way, we become more like him by knowing and loving him. However great our progress is in this life, it is far from that perfection by which God will be seen as he is, "face to face."[21] For then there will be such great perfection that love will possess much more than either faith has believed or hope has desired. May attainment discover more than thought has conceived! For that is the land of the living[22] and of those who see, of things which are perceived and understood, where truth is discerned without any bodily likeness nor obscured by clouds of any false opinions. There, as in the Trinity, which is God, the Father and the Son mutually see one another and their mutual vision consists in their being one and in the fact that the one is what the other is, so those who have been predestined for this and have been taken up into it will see God as he is, and in seeing him as he is they will become like him. And there, as in the Father and the Son, that which is vision is also unity; so in God and man that which is vision will be the likeness that is to come. The Holy Spirit, the unity of the Father and the Son, is himself the love and likeness of God and man.

6. But the manner is different for the supreme essence and for an inferior nature. For, in heaven, the splendor of the Lord will be seen,[23] not in a symbolic or a bodily way as it was seen on Mount Sinai[24] nor in a spiritual way as Isaiah[25] saw it or as John saw it in the Apocalypse,[26] but in a clear vision. The splendor of the Lord will not be seen dimly in a mirror[27] as it is seen in this life by men who are worthy of

20. Cf. Col 3:10.
21. 1 Cor 13:12; Par. 5 up to this point is borrowed from Augustine's *Ep.* 92.
22. Cf. Ps 26:13; 114:9.
23. Cf. Lk 2:9; Rev 21:11.
24. Ex 19:18ff.
25. Is 6:1-4.
26. Rev 1:9.
27. 1 Cor 13:12.

this vision — and then only to the degree that the soul of man can grasp it according to the grace it receives — but face to face.[28] But a person does not at all understand what he is seeking if he thinks that this can happen to a man still living this mortal life; that is, that a man by driving away and dispelling all clouds of bodily and carnal notions can possess the most serene light of unchanging truth, and that with his mind completely separated from everyday life, he can adhere to it continually and without change. Truly this pertains to the other life; and whoever wishes to possess in this world everything which should be possessed in the next, shows that he does not have faith. But merit accrues to the man who believes; reward is given to the man who sees.[29]

7. Therefore, let man rather believe especially the sublime and completely trustworthy authority which says that as long as we are in the body we are far from the Lord and walk by faith, not with a clear view.[30] And let a man who thus perseveringly holds on to and guards his faith, hope and love be intent upon this view, and let him do this through the pledge of the Holy Spirit[31] which we have received. For, he will teach us every truth[32] when God, "who has raised the Lord Jesus Christ from the dead, will give life also to our mortal bodies through his Spirit dwelling in us."[33] However, before God gives life, this body which is dead because of sin is without doubt corruptible and weighs down the soul.[34] When the soul, with the help it receives, rises above this cloud by which the whole earth is covered,[35] that is, this carnal darkness by which all earthly life is covered, it is struck as by a sudden flash of light and returns to its weakness keeping alive the desire to be raised again, but lacking sufficient purity

28. 1 Cor 13:12; up to this point Par. 6 is taken from Augustine's *De Genesi ad litteram* 12.
29. This sentence is Augustine's: *Tract. in Joh.* 68:3.
30. Cf. 2 Cor 5:6-7.
31. 2 Cor 1:22; 5:5.
32. Cf. Jn 16:13.
33. Rom 8:11.
34. Wis 9:15.
35. Sir 24:6.

to be held there. To the degree that someone is more able to remain there, he is greater; but to the degree that he is less able, he is inferior. But if until now the soul of a man, in which Christ dwells through faith,[36] has experienced nothing of this kind, the man must earnestly strive to diminish and mortify the desires of the flesh, of the eyes, and of the pride of this life.[37] With complete determination man must strengthen his faith through the action of moral virtue until he has been perfectly mortified by that death of which Moses spoke, "For man will not see me and live."[38] Then let man begin to live that life of which the Lord also speaks as he prays to God the Father for his disciples, "For this is eternal life, that they know you the one true God and Jesus Christ whom you have sent."[39]

8. Whoever has in Christ been awakened to God is stirred by the warmth of the Holy Spirit, and in his love for God has become small in his own eyes. He wishes to approach God, but cannot. And through the illumination God has given him, he fixes his gaze upon himself and finds that he and his sickness cannot be united with the purity of God. He finds it sweet to weep and to pray to God to have mercy on him again and again until he casts off all his affliction, to pray with confidence since he has already received, through no merit of his own, the pledge of salvation[40] through his only Savior, the Illuminator of man. Assuredly, knowledge does not puff up this man, needy and sorrowing, because love builds him up.[41] He has preferred one knowledge to another; he has preferred to know his own weakness more than to know the ramparts of the world, the foundations of the earth[42] and the heights of the heavens. And by increasing this knowledge he has increased sorrow,[43] the sorrow of his

36. Cf. Eph 3:17.
37. 1 Jn 2:16.
38. Ex 33:20.
39. Jn 17:3.
40. Cf. 2 Cor 1:22; 5:5.
41. 1 Cor 8:1.
42. Job 38:4.
43. Cf. Eccles 1:18.

earthly pilgrimage, because of his desire for his homeland and for his God, the blessed Creator.[44]

9. Lord my God, give me some of your bread, for I groan as a poor man among your poor, in the race of men, in the family of your Christ. I seek your face, Lord; I search for your face, Lord,[45] hungering and thirsting for your justice[46] in the contemplation of your face. Grant that I be filled with your truth, not with the fantasies of my heart lest I regress and fall into my own emptiness by rejecting your truth. I perceive clearly how many delusions the human heart can produce. And what is my heart but a human heart? But this I ask of you, God of my heart,[47] that none of these delusions cling to me in place of the real truth; but let the light of your truth come to me from that source from which the breath of Christ's truth is bestowed upon me, although I am cast far from the sight of your eyes[48] and am trying to return from afar by the way which you have prepared for us through the humanity of your only-begotten Son. Although I am subject to change I inhale this breath all the more gladly as I see in it nothing which is changeable either spatially or temporally as bodies are; neither subject to change only temporally and quasi-spatially such as the thoughts of our spirits; nor only temporally, with no spatial image at all, like certain reasonings of our minds. Indeed, your essence, by which you are what you are, has nothing in it that is changeable either in Eternity, in Trust, or in Will; because there truth is eternal and charity is true, and eternity is true and eternity is loved and truth is loved.[49]

10. For this reason, since we have been exiled from unchangeable joy — although not cut off or severed from it so that we do not even seek eternity, truth, or happiness in this mutable and temporal existence — and since we do not wish

44. All of Par. 8 is taken verbatim from *De trin.* 4:*prooem.*
45. Cf. Ps 26:8.
46. Cf. Mt 5:6.
47. Ps 72:26.
48. Cf. Ps 30:23.
49. All of Par. 9 is borrowed directly from *De trin.* 4:*prooem.*

to die or be deceived or be troubled, God has sent us means suitable to our journey by which we should be warned that what we seek does not exist in this life, but that we must return from this life to the next, and that if we do not give consideration to this, we are not seeking eternity, truth, and happiness in this life.[50] "When the fullness of time came, God sent his Son made of a woman, made under the law,"[51] so very lowly that he was "made," and clearly sent in the way in which he was "made." He came teaching marvels and marvelously persuading men to believe them: contempt of those things which are seen because of love for those things which are not seen, contempt for self because of love for God. He came doing unbelievable things, and more unbelievably teaching men that these must be believed.[52] The Lord Jesus Christ was humbled in order to teach us to be humble. He who contains all things was conceived; he who brings forth everything was born; he who gives life to all died. After three days he arose and ascended into heaven and placed at the right hand of the Father the human flesh he had assumed. This is marvelous, but it is far more marvelous that the whole world believed a thing so incredible.

11. If we consider the manner in which the world came to believe we see that this too is truly divine and most wonderful. Christ sent a very small number of fishermen with nets of faith to the sea of the world; they were uninstructed in the liberal arts and were completely untrained in what pertains to the world's teachings. They were not skilled in grammar nor armed with dialectic.[53] There were twelve of them and one of these turned back. Yet through these men he so filled the churches with every kind of fish that very many were signed with the cross on their foreheads even from among the wise men of the world to whom the cross of Christ seemed igno-

50. Thus far the paragraph is taken from *De trin.* 4:1.
51. Gal 4:4. This sentence is taken from *De trin.* 4:19.
52. The Latin for "teaching" is *contradens,* a Late Latin word.
53. Grammar and dialectic, together with rhetoric, make up the *trivium;* the *trivium* and the *quadrivium* (arithmetic, geometry, astronomy, and music) constituted the essentials upon which medieval education was based: the *artes liberales.* Grammar embraced the study of literature as well as language.

minious. What they considered an object of shame they placed on the pinnacle of honor. Therefore, when the whole world was sick, the Word of God veiled by the flesh came to men in this way to heal the world from its own destruction. He prepared medication with his own hands and spread it over the sicknesses of the world; this was the Gospel of the Kingdom, which was to be preached in the whole world, and the Scriptures of the Old and New Testaments, which are concerned with him. He gave as much authority to the Scriptures throughout the world as befitted the instrument through which God wished to be known to men and to be believed in by them. When men humbly entrust themselves to the Scriptures, they become subject to them. This is the faith through which those who are blessed with a pure heart are made clean.[54] To them is promised this vision which cannot be seen except by the pure of heart and which can be seen only if those who are to see it are purified through faith. We had to be cleansed since we were not fit to lay hold of eternal things and since we were weighed down with the squalor of sins contracted by the love of temporal things and implanted in us naturally, so to speak, from the root of our mortality. However, we could not be cleansed so as to be joined to eternal things except through the temporal things to which we were already joined and by which we were being held fast.[55] Because we are involved in temporal things and through love for them are held back from the eternal, a kind of temporal medicine undertakes to cure us, which calls to health, not those who know but those who believe. It has priority not by the excellence of its nature but by its order in time. Wherever a man falls there he must lie and there he must strive to get up again. Carnal forms hold us in their love into which we have lapsed through compliance with sin: to get up we must depend on them.[56] Therefore, the Son of

54. Cf. Mt 5:8.
55. These two sentences are from *De trin.* 4:18.
56. These sentences are from *De vera rel.* 24:45. In the next sentence following this section Augustine explains *formae carnales:* "I call those forms carnal which can be sensed through the flesh, that is through the eyes, the ears, and the other bodily senses."

God "who was in the form of God, emptied himself taking on the form of a servant,"[57] so that men, receiving by faith God who became man, might receive power to become sons of God.[58] Toward him who is present everywhere we are moved not spatially but through a striving for good and through good conduct.[59] And this we could not do if Wisdom did not condescend to become adapted to our great weakness and to offer us a model for living; and in no other way than through a man, since we ourselves are men. But because we act wisely when we approach this Wisdom, he is thought by proud men to have acted foolishly when he came to us. And since we become strong when we approach this Wisdom, it is, so to speak, weakened when it approaches us. But "the foolishness of God is wiser than men and his weakness is stronger than men."[60] Therefore, while God heals souls by every means suitable to the times, which he orders according to his marvelous wisdom, in no way has he cared for the human race more beneficently than when the Wisdom of God, that is, the only Son who is consubstantial and coeternal with the Father, condescended to assume a complete manhood.[61] "The Word was made flesh and dwelt among us."[62] Thus he demonstrated to men, who are carnal and unable to behold truth with their mind, and given over to carnal senses, how lofty a place human nature holds among creatures. For he appeared to men as a true man, and not merely in appearance; for he could have appeared in some ethereal body adapted to the ability of our sight. The very nature which

57. Phil 2:6-7.
58. Cf. Jn 1:12.
59. This is from *De doc. chr.* 1:10. Compare William's *Physics of the Soul,* 11: "... even if it does not move locally it does move through desire." —PL 180:720D; CF24.
60. 1 Cor 1:25; the previous passage is taken almost verbatim from *De doc. chr.* 1:11. The remainder of the paragraph is borrowed from *De vera rel.* 16:30.
61. The Latin for "complete manhood" is *totum hominem.* This terminology for the Incarnation— *homo* for human nature and *suscipere* or a synonym for the act of taking on a human nature—is traditional and is found throughout the *Enigma.* For the theological debate over *assumptus homo* see M.-D. Chenu, *Nature, Man and Society in the Twelfth Century* (Chicago, 1968) p. 286.
62. Jn 1:14.

was to be saved had to be assumed by him. And lest perhaps either sex should think that it was contemned by its Creator he assumed manhood born of a woman.

12. He did nothing by force, but everything by persuasion and instruction. The old servitude was truly past and a time of new freedom had dawned, and man for the sake of his salvation was being taught in a suitable way how he had been created with a free will. Through miracles he who was himself God promoted faith in God, and through his passion he elicited faith in the human nature which he bore. The people, devotees of pleasure, strove after riches to their ruin; he willed to be poor. They longed for honors and power; he refused to be king. They considered sons according to the flesh a great blessing; he spurned such wedlock and offspring. They were extremely proud and dreaded reproach; he endured every kind of insult. They thought injuries to be intolerable; what injury could be greater than that a just, innocent man be condemned? They cursed bodily pain; he was scourged and tortured. They feared death; he was punished with death. They thought the cross an ignominious kind of death; he was crucified. All the things we desired to have when we did not live right he showed to be of no value by doing without them. All that we wished to avoid and which caused us to turn away from zeal for godliness, he bore patiently and made powerless. No sin can be committed which does not involve seeking after what he despised or fleeing from what he endured. Thus his whole life on earth, through the humanity which he condescended to assume, was an instruction in living righteously.[63] When these things are believed without hesitation and in faith are pondered in order to love what is believed and to see it as it is believed, what is this but the purification of the heart to see what is promised to the pure of heart? [64]

63. Par. 12 to here is from *De vera rel.* 16:31.
64. Cf. Mt 5:8; the Latin here contains the compound *mundicors,* pure of heart, which occurs many times in Augustine. Augustine borrowed the word from an Old Latin version of Mt 5:8 as exemplified by his *De trin.* 8:4: *Beati enim mundicordes, quia ipsi deum videbunt.*

13. But Divine Providence not only watches over men separately or individually, it also watches over the whole human race as a community. What is done in individual cases is known by God himself, for he is the one who does it, and by the persons involved. But what is done with the human race God wished to be preserved through history and through prophecy.[65] Faith must be placed in both of these so that each member of the faithful can entrust his spirit faithfully to God both because of what he as an individual has received from God and what he together with mankind has received. Faith in things in time whether visible or invisble, has greater strength through belief than through understanding.[66] For, unless a man believes what is said he can in no way be convinced of it. Thus,[67] the basis for our following this religion is the history and prophecy of the temporal dispensation of Divine Providence concerning the transformation and redemption undertaken for the salvation of mankind unto eternal life. When these facts are believed the soul will be purged by a way of life reconciled to God's teachings and in conformity with the examples he has given us. Also such a manner of living will make the soul suitable to grasp spiritual truths which have neither past nor future but always remain the same and are not susceptible to change; that is, the one God himself, Father, Son, and Holy Spirit.

14. As a matter of fact, since they have gone by in time, it is only by faith that we know things which could be seen in the past.[68] And we do not hope for them as things still to be seen, but believe them as things done and completed, as is the case with the statement, "Christ died once for our sins and arose."[69] This expresses a fact which is not hoped for as something of the future, but rather loved as something accom-

65. Thus far Par. 13 is borrowed from *De vera rel.* 15:46. The expression "through history and through prophecy" refers to the historical books of the OT and the OT books of prophecies.

66. This sentence occurs in *De vera rel.* 15:46.

67. The remainder of Par. 13 is taken from *De vera rel.* 7:13.

68. All of Par. 14-17, and 18 up to the quotation from Rom 1:20 are borrowed from Augustine, Ep 120:2.

69. Cf. 1 Pet 3:18; 1 Cor 15:3-4.

plished. But those things that are not as yet, but will be, are believed in such a way that they are hoped for as something to be seen and are also loved, such as the resurrection of our spiritual bodies,[70] though they can in no way be manifested now. But of those things which exist such that they have neither past nor future but endure forever, some are invisible, such as wisdom and justice; some are visible, such as the body of Christ already immortal. But invisible things are seen when they are understood[71] and in this way are seen in some manner which is suited to them. And when they are seen, they are much more certain than those things which are experienced through the senses of the body. But things are called invisible because they cannot at all be seen by these bodily eyes. Things which remain visible can be seen even by these bodily eyes if they are brought into view. Thus the Lord showed himself to the disciples after the Resurrection,[72] and to the apostle Paul and the deacon Stephen after the Ascension.[73]

15. Likewise, we believe in those things that remain permanently visible in such a way that even if they are not shown to us, we hope some day we shall see them. We do not try to understand them with our reason or our intellect; except that, since they are visible, we mentally distinguish them from invisible things and picture them as they appear to us in our thoughts, although frequently they differ from the way we imagine them. But justice and wisdom and other such things we do not conceive of in one way and behold in another; rather, we look upon these invisible things which we know through the attention of our mind and reason without any shape or bodily mass, without any features and delineation of parts, and without any spatial limits or unlimited expanse.[74] And similarily we gaze upon the very light by

70. Cf. 1 Cor 15-40, 44.
71. Cf. Rom 1:20.
72. Cf. Lk 24:40; Jn 20:20.
73. Cf. Acts 9:3-5; 7:55.
74. In this long passage from Augustine the phrase "unlimited expanse" renders the Latin *spatiis infinitis.* See Augustine, *De civitate dei* 12:13 for *infinita tempora.* Thomas Aquinas discusses the question of *spatium infinitum* in his *Commentaria in octo libros physicorum Aristotelis* 3:7.

which we distinguish all these things, the image of eternal reason,[75] in which there appears to us in a satisfactory way what it is we believe without knowing and what we possess as known; what shape we call to mind through the senses of the body; what shape we fashion with our thoughts; what touches the senses of the body; what the mind imagines as corporeal; what the intelligence looks upon as certain but completely unlike all corporeal things. Now, as all these things are discerned, this light is not diffused all around and localized in space like the brightness of the sun and the other physical lights. It illumines our mind as if with a visible brilliance, but shines invisibly and in an ineffable manner, but nevertheless intelligibly; it is as certain for us as the fact that it renders certain for us all those things we see through its instrumentality.

16. There are, therefore, three kinds of things which are seen: one is coporeal, such as sky and earth and whatever there is in them which the bodily senses perceive and come in contact with; the second is similar to the corporeal, such as those things which we think about with our spirit and picture to ourselves or which we look upon as the recollection or impression of a corporeal reality. From here come those visions which occur as if with physical substance in dreams or in some disturbances of the mind. The third kind is different from the other two because it is not corporeal and has no similarity to the corporeal; for example, wisdom, which is perceived and understood by the mind, and by whose light a true judgment is made concerning all these other things.

FAITH IN THE TRINITY

17. In which of these three classes should we believe God the Trinity to be? For, it is the Trinity we wish to know about. Obviously, it is in one of them or in none. If in one, it is clearly in that which is superior to the other two, as wisdom is. But if we possess wisdom as his gift and it is less than that supreme and unchangeable wisdom which is spoken

75. The phrase "the image of the eternal reason" is inserted by William into this section of Augustine.

of as the Wisdom of God,[76] I think we should not consider
the Giver inferior to his gift. But if we possess some of his
splendor, which is called our wisdom, in so far as we can
grasp anything of the Trinity in a mirror dimly,[77] we must
distinguish it from all bodies and from all bodily things.

18. But if it is necessary to say that the Trinity belongs to
none of these classes, and is so invisible as not to be seen even
by the mind, we have much less reason to hold such an
opinion about it as to believe it to be similar to corporeal
things or to the likenesses of coporeal things. It does not
surpass corporeal things by its beauty or its great size, but by
the difference and distinctness of its nature. And if it is beyond comparison with our spiritual goods, such as justice,
wisdom, charity, and others like them, which we certainly do
not value for their pysical size nor imagine with some kind of
corporeal form, but rather, when we understand them correctly, look upon them in the light of our mind without any
bodily substance or bodily likeness, how much more is the
Trinity above comparison with all quantities and qualities!
Still, the Apostle is a witness that it is not entirely removed
from our understanding when he says, "His invisible attributes are seen for they are understood through the things
which have been made; also his everlasting power and divinity."[78] Consequently, although we labor through knowledge
to grasp the Trinity in those things which touch our bodily
senses or to understand what we ourselves are in our spiritual
nature and we fail, nevertheless faithful devotion does not
burn impudently in us for those divine, ineffable things that
are above us. Pride in our own resources does not inflate this
devotion, but grace and a desire for the Creator and Re-
deemer enkindle it. But let man consider that there is nothing
in his nature which is better than his own intellect by which
he desires to understand God. And let him see whether he

76. Cf. 1 Cor 2:7.
77. 1 Cor 13:12.
78. Rom 1:20. With this sentence from Romans the long passage borrowed
from Augustin's *Ep.* 120 concludes. The remainder of Par. 18 is taken from *De
trin.* 5:1.

sees there any indication of shapes, brightness of colors, immensity of space, distinction of parts, distention of mass, any movement through intervals of space, or anything of this kind. For certainly we find nothing of the kind in that faculty which is the highest in our nature, our intellect. For it is with our intellect that we grasp wisdom itself to the degree that we are capable of doing so. Therefore, what we do not find in our highest faculty we should not consider to be in that which is so incomparably superior to it.

19. But the force of love is so great that what the human mind has thought about with love for a long time and has adhered to with the bond of concern, it draws along with it, even when it returns to itself or turns toward that which is above it: the divine nature.[79] And because it has loved deeply through the senses of the body those corporeal entities which are external to it and has become implicated with them by a long-standing association, and yet cannot bring them within with itself, as it were, into the realm of incorporeal nature, the human mind brings along with it images of these things, imagining itself, or the divine nature mentioned above, as existing in the same way in which it must think of them.

20. Lord God, this is the curse with which you cursed the earth in the work of Adam and his sons; when they toil on the land it does not yield its fruit for them but puts forth thorns and thistles so that they eat their bread in the sweat of their brow.[80] And what will your little ones do, sons of man, they who are not so much earthly dwellers from the earth as heavenly dwellers from heaven, men of your right hand whom you have chosen for yourself, "who already have the first-fruits of the spirit and thus are awaiting the redemption of their bodies"? [81] For they groan within themselves, already long-since freed from sin but not yet from the

79. All of Par. 19 is taken from *De trin.* 10:5. For "the force of love" I am following the Uppsala C. 79 reading *vis amoris* on f. 62ᵛ of that manuscript. Charleville 114, f. 84ᵛ, reads *vis moris,* force of habit. However, the Uppsala reading agrees with the manuscript tradition of Augustine's text which is William's source here.

80. Cf. Gen 3:14-19.

81. Rom 8:23.

punishment of sin. Because of the punishment of the first
sinner they go forth in sorrow to scatter their seeds,[82] and
although they live from your table they scarcely ever receive
their daily bread from your hand except after tearful labor
and the sting of compunction. Living bread[83] which gives
them life is the memorial of your abundant sweetness,[84] the
grace of your visitation and of a kind of vision of you, and
joy in the feeling of your love and your goodness. Now, while
the world rejoices, you permit these to weep and mourn,
promising to others desolation, but to these consolation.[85]
You wish them to hunger and thirst, but you promise them
everlasting abundance.[86] You impose a delay to try their
love, yet you accord them an abundance of your visits and
the sight of you to comfort them in this delay. And when
you find a will and intention which is pure through pre-
venient grace, in the very hour of your visit you perfect
purity in the soul of the faithful by virtue of your presence
and your bountiful grace. And purity merits vision according
to its capacity, but as the Apostle says, "in part"[87] and
"dimly in a mirror."[88] As long as they are exiled in the flesh
away from you their Lord God,[89] they lack the ability to see
you, except in part,[90] inasmuch as there still exists in them in
part that which must first die. This the Lord testifies to those
striving perfectly to see you face to face, as you are,[91] when
he says to Moses, "Man will not see me and live."[92]

21. What is that but our sinful body, our body of
concupiscences of the flesh which naturally grow in us? It is
from this that he so anxiously and tearfully kept asking to be
freed, who said, "Unhappy man that I am, who will free me

82. Cf. Ps 125:6.
83. Jn 6:51.
84. Ps 144:7.
85. Cf. Jn 16:20.
86. Cf. Mt 5:6.
87. 1 Cor 13:9.
88. 1 Cor 13:12.
89. Cf. 2 Cor 5-6.
90. Cf. 1 Cor 13:12.
91. Cf. 1 Jn 3:2.
92. Ex 33:20.

from the body of this death? The grace of God through our
Lord Jesus Christ."[93] Now the person saying this did not
desire bodily death through impatience with life, but he
desired freedom from certain concupiscences of the flesh
which were still alive in him and from which no one liberates
except the grace of God through our Lord Jesus Christ by the
diffusion of his love in our hearts through the Holy Spirit
whom he gives us.[94] This is the law of the spirit of life,
freeing, as the same Apostle says, "from the law of sin and
death";[95] that is, the concupiscences of the flesh. These are
like dirt in the interior eye of man keeping him from seeing
that which is seen only by the pure of heart and from eternal
life of which the Lord says, "This is eternal life, that they
know you the true God and Jesus Christ whom you have
sent."[96] So that the interior eye which is made to see God
can see in the next life, it is cleansed in this life where that
vision begins which is perfected in the next. It begins here
with a holy life and by the pursuit of the contemplation of
God; for here love merits vision when that which is not seen
is believed in, hoped for, and loved. The vision is to be perfected in the next life where it will nourish love. Then every
virtue will consist in loving what will be possessed, and complete happiness will consist of possessing what will be loved.
This is why the Apostle, who was such a man as we have been
discussing, and those who are now such men say, "I wish to
be set free and to be with Christ, for that is a much better
thing."[97] Men such as these walk in faith[98] and even if they
are perfect, they are travellers;[99] they have not yet reached
the end of their journey. They are perfect in that they have
forgotten what is behind them and push on to what lies

93. Rom 7:24-25.
94. Cf. Rom 5:5.
95. Cf. Rom 8:2.
96. Jn 17:3.
97. Phil 1:23.
98. Cf. 2 Cor 5:7.
99. The terminology *viatores* and *perventores* occurs again in Par. 39. This is
traditional terminology and is found in Augustine, *De peccatorum meritis et
remissione* 2:13 and Gregory the Great, *Hom. in evangelia* 1:14.

ahead; they are travellers in that they are still on a journey.

22. "Lord God of my heart, and my portion forever,"[100] the goal of all my desire and the object of my attention, among these men, although by far inferior to them and in ways different from theirs, I have now for a long time made progress along the journey, walking toward you by faith, in order to live right. And I have made progress in purifying my heart to see you and contemplate you. I have grown old in this endeavor and still have not yet begun.[101] Often, I think about our common faith in you without which it is impossible to please you, the Lord our God, and in which you have established the salvation of all, and thus that faith is necessary for all, both the very lowly and the great in the Church of God. And then I consider how, when knowledge of faith is sought among the holy doctors, it is found involved with such a great perplexity of questions and obscured by such enigmatic disputes that its purity can scarcely be apprehended by even a few men. It at times seems good to return to that earliest, most happy, golden time of evangelical simplicity and to that particular style of your Holy Spirit through which the law of the spirit of life[102] was first inscribed on the human hearts of believers through the ministry of those who could foresee that your only-begotten Son, our Savior, was to come in the flesh, or of those who merited to see him come.

23. When I found everything clear in the Scriptures which were common both to the wise and to the simple, and which engaged the strong in such a way as not to frighten away the weak, then I recalled the prophets, reproach to the Jewish people for despising the waters of Shiloah[103] which flowed silently in their own country and for journeying to Egypt to

100. Ps 72:26.
101. The Latin is *in hoc consenui et nondum cepi.* The *Enigma of Faith* was written between 1140 and approximately 1145, but since the exact date of William's birth is disputed his age at the time of writing this treatise can only be estimated. See the *Letter to Haymo,* written after 1144, where William says he is "an old man and tottering" (CF 12, p. 7).
102. Rom 8:2. For the expression *stilum Spiritus sancti tui* see Davy, *Théologie et mystique de Guillaume de Saint-Thierry* (Paris, 1954) pp. 94-96.
103. Cf Is 8:6.

drink the turgid waters of the river of Egypt.[104] We are not
constrained to purchase our water there with money, as some
complain through another prophet, nor "to give a hand to
Egypt and Assyria so that we may be filled with bread";[105]
rather, we receive all things free. Divine authority, which it is
wrong to contradict, stands ready there to aid everyone
saying, "Only believe and you will be saved."[106] And, "All
things are possible to one who believes."[107] Therefore,[108]
Lord our God, we hear you there speaking the truth,
"Go, baptize every nation in the name of the Father,
and of the Son, and of the Holy Spirit,"[109] and immediately
we believe in you, Father, Son, and Holy Spirit. Truth would
not say this if you were not this. Nor would you have ordered us to be baptized, Lord God, in the name of one who was
not Lord and God; and not in the name but in the names, if
you, Father, Son, and Holy Spirit, were not one God. For it
would not have been proclaimed by the voice of God, "Hear,
Israel, the Lord your God is one God,"[110] if you were not
one God, you who are Father, Son, and Holy Spirit. And if
you, God the Father, were yourself your Son, your Word,
Christ, and if you yourself were your gift and the gift of your
Son, the Holy Spirit, we would not read in the Words of
truth, "God sent his own Son,"[111] nor would you, the only-
begotten Son, speak of the Holy Spirit who proceeds from
the Father and from you, "Whom the Father will send in my
name,"[112] and "Whom I will send you from the Father."[113]
Therefore it is not the Father himself who is the Son, nor the
Son himself who is the Holy Spirit. With my whole attention
directed on this rule of faith, Lord, I will seek your face and

104. Cf. Jer 2:18.
105. Lam 5:6.
106. Cf. Lk 8:50.
107. Cf. Mk 9:22.
108. The remainder of Par. 23 has its source in *De trin.* 15:28.
109. Mt 28:19.
110. Deut 6:4.
111. Cf. Jn 3:17; Gal 4:4.
112. Jn 14:26.
113. Jn 15:26.

continually search for your face[114] as much as I can and as much as you render me capable of doing. Lord my God, my one hope, hear me lest exhausted I lose the will to seek you. May I ardently seek you always. Give the strength to seek, you who have given the desire. And when the strength is sufficient, add to the desire which you have given. May I always remember you, understand you, and love you until, faithfully remembering you and prudently understanding you and truthfully loving you, O Triune God, according to the fullness which you know, you reform me to your image in which you created me.

24. Therefore, I have here everything concerning the Lord my God which I was searching for for some time. I have it free of tormenting questions, insidious sophistry, and noisy arguments; namely, what it is that the Father is, the Son is, and the Holy Spirit is. This is my faith about God because it is the Catholic faith.[115] I believe what I read or hear because he, who calls himself Truth, has instructed me to believe it. For, he said, "Whoever believes will be saved. But who does not believe will be condemned."[116] And what is believed if not the Truth which is the Lord Jesus Christ? A man is not a Christian who is unwilling to believe him and to believe in him. I openly confess that I am a Christian. I believe him whom I believe in. And I believe his Scriptures through which I am confident I will have life. This is the foundation which the Wisdom of God has ordained,[117] the Word of God has proclaimed, and which the Apostles, like wise builders, have put in place. And whoever wishes to add to it should examine what he is adding; however, he can be sure of the foundation, for the foundation will stand.[118] However, what is added will be tested by fire; but as to the composition of the founda-tion, he who made it will see to that.

---

114. Cf. Ps 26:8. This was a favorite text of William, one that he used very frequently. He was facinated by the "face of God." See CF 3:100-101, n. 37.

115. See *De trin.* 1:5 for this same statement.

116. Mk 16:16.

117. For this building imagery see 1 Cor 3:10-11.

118. 2 Tim 2:19.

25. Now, why do I seek what cannot be known in this life?
For example, why do I seek to know how the Trinity in
heaven can be a unity, or how three can be one; since the
Lord and the Apostles and the prophets before them taught
that this is the nature of the Lord our God, and added nothing more than this? If the Word and Wisdom of God had
wished us to know this in this life, no one could have taught
it better in this world than he, through himself or through his
Apostles. I can say with confidence that even our holy Fathers, doctors of the Church after the Apostles, could have
said nothing more if they had been permitted to speak. For
as long as they were able, they wished to add nothing beyond
this. We can go through the entire list of the canonical Scriptures, both Old and New Testaments, and as for the name
"Trinity," nowhere do we read that God is a Trinity. And
nowhere is it to be found even that they are three: Father,
Son, and Holy Spirit; except in the Epistle of John where it is
said, "There are three who bear witness in heaven, the Father, the Word, and the Holy Spirit; and these three are
one."[119] However, even this is lacking in the ancient translation.[120]

26. But I say this only about the name and number, not
about the interpretation or understanding of the Trinity. Just
as has already been said, all the Scriptures declare that God
the Father, and God the Son, and God the Holy Spirit are
one God. However, nowhere are there mentioned three persons in the Divinity, nowhere is there mentioned the relation
of these persons, nowhere the celebrated name for consubstantiality, *homoousion*, or even the name of simple sub-

119. 1 Jn 5:7. William apparently forgot Mt 28:19, but this is curious since he
quoted this verse in Par. 23 above. In any case William seems to base his statement
on that of *De trin.* 7:4, "We do not find three persons mentioned anywhere in
Scriptures." However, Augustine is speaking of the absence of the words "three
persons" not simply the mention of three in one God.
120. 1 Jn 5:7 is the so-called Johannine comma. The earliest inclusion of this
verse in the NT occurs in the fourth century in the *Liber apologeticus* by Instan-
tius, a disciple of Priscillus of Avila. See A. Robert and A. Feuillet, *Introduction
to the New Testament* (New York, 1965) pp. 683-685. The source for William's
awareness of the lack of the Johannine comma in the earliest versions of the Bible
has eluded discovery.

stance, nowhere the category of relation,[121] nor the other categories. But when heresies began to arise in the Church, against novelty in terminology and interpretation these words or names and others of this kind were invented in the cause of the faith; however, without changing the ancient interpretations and without falsifying the canonical Scriptures. Because of this, these names were accepted by all the faithful with even the same authority and reverence with which they accepted from ancient times the names of Father, Son, and Holy Spirit, and all the other ancient names of these realities of which all these names are signs. With the Divine Names or whatever words are used to say something about God, attention must be given not so much to the signs themselves of the names or words, as to that which is designated through these signs. The time was at hand to sift the Catholic faith in order to purify it;[122] to practice it in order to test it. And for this reason the ineffable nature of the Highest Good has rather indulgently allowed himself to be lowered into human words to help man in his devotion towards God; not, however, so much that he is confined by human reason. Since words of this kind are instruments of common reason concerning common realities, they are nothing but scandals when they are used in the cause of the faith, unless they are adapted faithfully to the reasoning of faith. [123] The great Lord and his Wisdom which is without number[124] have not refused a name implying number, "Trinity," in that it is simply stated that God is Father, God is Son, and God is Holy Spirit. Likewise, he has not refused that new name, *homoousion*, by which those who are Father, Son, and Holy Spirit are said to be one

---

121. The Latin is *ad aliquid* for "the category of relation." This is one of the ten categories of being; these categories or predicaments can be found in Boethius, *De trin.* 4: "There are a total of ten predicaments which are universally predicated of all things; they are substance, quality, quantity, relation, place, time, condition, situation, activity, and passivity." See Pars. 29 and 30 where William deals with these.

122. Cf. 1 Cor 11:19.

123. "Reason of faith" translates *ratio fidei.* See the introductory section on William's sources for a discussion of this expression. This is the first occurrence of the expression in the treatise.

124. Cf. Ps 146:5.

God; the one name designating what they each are, the other designating what they are in relation to one another and that they are one.

27. Before Sabellius[125] rose up in the Church preaching that he is the Father who is the Son, and that he is the Holy Spirit who is the Father or the Son, the preaching of the faith concerning the Father, Son, and Holy Spirit had no need of the name "Trinity." When this name was taken up in the cause of the faith and people began to speak of three, Father, Son, and Holy Spirit, they also began to ask what these three were. Neither then nor up to the present has an answer been found to express this reality correctly. Indeed, what is said with "three persons" is another thing which will be spoken of later. Likewise, before Arius rose up who by adding inequality and dissimilarity tried to inflict on us a crowd of gods, the reasoning of faith was unaware of the word *homoousion* although the sense of the name was not unknown to it, for it preached this from the beginning. Could the faithful of that time be ignorant of what the Lord said, "I and the Father are one"? [126] This is *homoousion* and nothing else.

28. As we have already said, the name is new and circumstances necessitated its use in the preaching of the faith; however, the reality is the same. Therefore, just as the name of "Trinity" was admitted in the cause of the faith against Sabellius, so, *homoousion*, the name of consubstantiality, was set up against Arius. And thus, number, if indeed it is number, was discovered or assumed in that nature which is the Creator of all things, which even created the weight, measure, and number, in which it distributed everything it created.[127] But what is this number? What sort of thing is it? It is not increasing, nor diminishing; not separating, nor joining together; not dividing, nor confounding. It is not true that, as

125. William mentions Sabellius several times in the treatise. Compare his criticism of William of Conches in *On the Errors of William of Conches*, PL 180:337B. Abelard had been accused of Sabellianism by some of his critics. See Luscombe, *The School of Peter Abelard* (Cambridge, 1969) p. 104, n. 6 and p. 188.

126. Jn 10:30.

127. Cf. Wisdom 11:21.

in a trinity of three men there are three men, so in the Trinity three gods must be considered or reckoned. For, there those who are three are one; those who are one are three. One does not make up a third part of this Trinity; nor are two a greater part than one; nor are three together something greater than each one individually, for the magnitude is spiritual, not corporeal. The three in the Trinity, therefore, as if because of the perfection of each, are not parts of the one God; likewise, we must not conclude or consider that there are three gods whether perfect or imperfect. Then, where is number? The number which is there is number and is not number. There is something there which is ineffable and which cannot be explained with words. For, when you say "Father, Son, and Holy Spirit," three seem to be enumerated; but there is no number there. If you ask what the three are, number fails. When you begin to think about the Trinity, you begin to count; when you have enumerated you cannot answer what it is you have enumerated; for, each individually is God in the Trinity. Are there three gods? Heaven forbid! Each individually is omnipotent. Are there three who are omnipotent? By no means. There are not three gods, nor three who are omnipotent, nor three wisdoms, nor three who are wise, nor three who are great, nor three who have grandeur.[128] All these things are said of God substantially. And so great is the power of that supreme substance in the Father, the Son, and the Holy Spirit, that whatever is said about each one individually is not to be taken in the plural collectively, but is to be taken in the singular. For, we speak of God the Father, God the Son, and God the Holy Spirit, but we do not say that collectively there are three gods, but one.[129]

---

128. William here parallels certain passages from the *Quicumque* Symbol, esp. Sections 13-14:

Similiter omnipotens Pater, omnipotens
Filius, omnipotens Spiritus Sanctus;
et tamen non tres omnipotentes, sed
unus omnipotens.

Augustine uses similar expressions in *De trin.* 5:8 and 7:3. William may have used either Augustine or the Symbol as a source here.

129. The previous two sentences are from *De trin.* 5:8. See Par. 46 for the same passage.

29. And this is the general rule of all names, not only those which have been pointed out as spoken substantially of God, but even of those which are said of God in reference to creation, such as Creator, Lord, and others like these. For things of this kind, such as magnitude, goodness, and so forth, according as they are in things, are accidents; but they are not accidents in God. For, when these are said of God, we must understand him, to the degree that we can, as good, without quality; big, without quantity; Creator, without a need to create; present, without being limited to one place; containing all things, without himself having an external form; totally everywhere, without location; eternal, without time; making mutable things, without change in himself; and without passivity.[130] When one asks concerning the Father, and the Son, and the Holy Spirit what these three are, he does not ask this about that which they are in relation to one another, but about that which they are. You can no more speak of three good or three great or anything of this sort than you can speak of three gods according to the above-mentioned rule of the substantial names of God.[131]

30. But human weakness which is infected by the habitual use of numbers and things which can be enumerated insists and says: everything which is said to be relative to something else, is also something unto itself beyond that which is said to be relative to something else. For example, there are three men: a father, a son, and some friend of theirs. In that they are something in themselves, they are men; in that they are something in relation to each other they are father, son and friend. If they were not that which they are in themselves, they could not be that which they are in relation to each other. Thus, those who are Father, Son, and Holy Spirit in

---

130. This sentence is drawn from *De trin.* 5:1; see also *De trin.* 1:1. In addition, compare *De natura corporis et animae* 2, PL 180:791CD and 720A. The phrase "without himself having an external form" translates *sine habitu. Habitus* or *habere* is one of the ten categories of being; see note 121 above for the categories. *Habitus* cannot be translated by a single word; the phrase *sine habitu* means something like "without possessing anything external to himself." Chenu, *Introduction à l'étude de Saint Thomas d'Aquin* (Paris, 1950) p. 87, points out the difficulty of dealing with this word.

131. See the end of Par. 28 and the beginning of Par. 29.

relation to one another are three entities or three persons in themselves. What are the three persons? What are the three entities? If no response is made here, Sabellius has demonstrated that for which he is called a heretic. The supereminence of the Divinity exceeds every ability of our common speech.[132] If we consider the reality as it is, without a doubt it is Father, it is Son, it is Holy Spirit; and he is not Son who is Father nor is he Holy Spirit who is Father and Son. Thus there are three. Someone will ask, "Are there three essences? " Heaven forbid! For, according to the above-mentioned rule of Divine Names,[133] the essence is Father, the essence is Son, and the essence is Holy Sprit; but still there are not three essences, there is only one essence. Then what are the three persons? Human words fail, so let us fly to the words of the Word. When the Lord spoke to the Jews about himself and about his Father they said, "Where is your Father? ";[134] as if they were saying, "You say there are two, you and your Father; we see you, where is your Father? " The Lord answers, "I and the Father are one";[135] as if he were saying "We are (because I and the Father are two) one (because I am one God with the Father.[136]

31. Therefore, just as the Lord, when he was asked, said that he and the Father were one; so also, we, who have been taught by him concerning the Trinity which is God, answer "One" to that person asking what the three entities are and what the three beings are. If he is impudent and still persists in asking what the one is, we say "One God." But if he is a man of faith, he will not be so impudent as to continue and ask who God is, since there is no God but the one God: Father, Son, and Holy Spirit. Therefore, it is not true that the Father and the Son "is" one, as Sabellius says; but "are" one, as the Lord says.[137] Also, if the Holy Spirit were not

132. The last four sentences echo *De trin.* 7:4.
133. See the end of Par. 28 and the beginning of Par. 29.
134. Jn 8:19,
135. Jn 10:30.
136. Compare Augustine's phrasing of this same idea in *De trinn.* 7:6.
137. William's source for this sentence is *De trin* 5:9.

God as expressed by *homoousion*, that is, of the same substance with the Father and the Son, the Lord would by no
means say, "The Spirit is God."[138] And elsewhere, "If I cast
out devils through the Spirit of God. . . ."[139] Likewise, "The
Lord and his Spirit have sent me."[140] And all the Scriptures
agree on this point, that the Holy Spirit is one God with the
Father and the Son. And this is the one thing, or the only
thing which David asks of the Lord and seeks to contemplate
saying, "I ask one thing of the Lord, this I shall seek."[141] But
this "only thing" is not one in number, but in nature, that is,
a solid entity,[142] without parts; but in everything which it is
or which it possesses it has its own complete integrity—if
"everything" or "complete" or "integrity" can be said of
something which has no parts. However, wherever in the
Scriptures many things are spoken of as one, and no mention
is made of what that one is, as is done with the phrase "one
heart and one mind,"[143] the same nature is signified which is
in no way dissimilar or differing. Therefore, in proportion as
three things exist in this way they are one. But, for three
things to exist in this way is a characteristic of the Trinity
alone, which is God. For even if there were ever three men
with the same nature and with the same will or who were in
accord, it is certain that three men would always be three
men. And if ever they agreed in some things, they would
disagree in many things. But in the Trinity which is God,
those who are three are very truly one; and they are not three

138. Jn 4:24.
139. Lk 11:20.
140. Is 48:16.
141. Ps 26:4. The distinction William is making is clearer in the Latin. "The one
thing, or the only thing" translates *hec est una, vel hoc est unum.* The Vulgate for
Ps 26:4 is *Unam petii a Domino, hanc requiram.* See Jerome, *in Zachariam
prophetam* 3:14 where this psalm verse occurs with the reading *Unum petivi a
Domino, hoc requiram.* Also, see Jerome, *Enarratio secunda in ps. 26* 2:6 where he
discusses the use of the feminine in the version *unam petii a Domino.* Finally,
Jerome, *Commentarioli in psalmos* discusses this under Ps 26:6-9.
142. "A solid entity" renders *solidum idipsum.* For the full connotation of the
word *idipsum* see *De trin.* 3:2, "*Idipsum* is here understood as the supreme and
unchangeable Good." Also, see William's *Disputatio adv. Abaelardum* 2 for
another example of *idipsum* with this pregnant meaning.
143. Acts 4:32.

gods but one God of one nature and the same essence. And predication of one essence implies perfect unity. Therefore when someone asks about the Father, the Son, and the Holy Spirit, whether they are three and what the three are, on the authority of the Lord and in accordance with the reasoning of faith, there is no better answer nor one closer to the truth than that they are one.

32. Because of the necessity for examination or the difficulty of treatment or discussion, the Fathers decided to allow a plural number, except for relative names. And to respond with one name to the question of what the three were, they decided to speak of "three persons," but in such a way that no mass is implied in the Trinity, no space, no difference of any kind of dissimilarity whatsoever, no separable distinction or confusion of persons. Let neither part nor whole be implied here. The Trinity is not something greater than one person, nor is a person less than the whole Trinity.[144] Although they may appear to be distinguished one from the other; nevertheless, as faith can understand it, it must be understood that these three who are spoken of as three persons are infinite in themselves, that each one is in each, and each one is in all, and all are in all, and all are one.[145] Either through devout faith or through some kind of understanding, Catholic devotion has been afraid to speak of three essences with respect to the Lord its God lest any diversity be understood in that Supreme Equality; and this has been the case whenever human indigence has tried to express this ineffable reality to the degree that it has been able to grasp it in the depths of its mind, and to present it to the understanding of men. This is the reality which we have tried to express almost ineffably, relying on the interpretations and terminology of the holy Fathers.[146] Indeed, this is a truth known with

144. For the previous sentences see *De trin.* 6:10.
145. This sentence has its source in *De trin.* 6:10. Compare the end of Par. 48 below.
146. The previous two sentences are taken from *De trin.* 1:1 and 7:4. William uses Augustine's mode of contradictory expression here when trying to speak of the unspeakable Mystery: *ineffabile . . . ineffabiliter fari.* See Par. 41 below where a parallel statement occurs.

great certitude from the Scriptures and which must devoutly be believed and upon which even the focus of the mind is held: that there exists one who is the Father, and one who is the Son, and one who is the Holy Spirit; and that the same one who is the Son is not the Father nor is he the Holy Spirit who is the Son or the Father.

33. Nevertheless, since Catholic devotion did not dare speak of three essences, it asked what it could say without the least offense, and spoke of three persons. It did not wish diversity to be understood by these names, but it did not wish singularity lest God be understood as being single. Three persons are so spoken of, that unity alone will not be understood in the Trinity, and in order that some kind of response may be made in an ordinary way of speaking.[147] Even if the Trinity, as it really is, cannot be spoken about, still it is not altogether passed over when one says what the three entities or three beings are.[148] In addition, through these names for the three persons there are provided for all the faithful, facilities for speaking about the Ineffable which are more expressive and more succinct both for responding more carefully to adversaries, for making more precise inquiries about God, and for conferring with friends. Also, the confession of faith now has a form of sound terminology and a verbal instrument fit for exposition or disputation.

34. Those who define "person" define it in two ways, either as the individual substance of a rational nature;[149] or that of which, by its form, there is certain knowledge.[150] The first

147. The end of Par. 32 and the beginning of Par. 33 are taken from *De trin.* 7:4. See the end of Par. 47 for the same passage paraphrased. William uses some of this passage in *On the Errors of William of Conches*, PL 180:336C; he identifies it as Augustine's in this latter work.

148. The same sentence occurs in William's treatise against William of Conches, PL 180:337B where the author attributes it to Augustine. See *De trin.* 5:9 and 7:6.

149. For the definition of person as the individual substance of a rational nature see Boethius, *Liber de persona et duabus naturis*, PL 64:1343CD. This was the standard definition for "person" throughout the Middle Ages. See E. K. Rand, *Founders of the Middle Ages* (New York, 1928) p. 150.

150. The second definition of person given by William is taken from Boethius also. See *Liber de persona*, PL 64:1343D-1344A where the phrase occurs:

definition, which employs the name of substance in its expression, is not an ambiguous concept; clearly it is of a kind with those names which are spoken of God substantially and absolutely, such as when it is said that the Father is God, the Son is God, and the Holy Spirit is God, and still there are not three gods, but one God.[151] Thus, if person is predicated of God, let the Father be called a person, the Son a person, and the Holy Spirit a person, but in all let it be said that there is one person. And according to this definition it is no more proper to speak of three persons in the Trinity than to speak of three gods. Next, according to the second definition, when we are asked what the three are, we answer "three persons"; since each one of them, from the form of the expression by which is said either "the person of the Father," or "the person of the Son," or "the person of the Holy Spirit," offers knowledge of himself which is certain and each has some ability to answer what the three are. The answer is given with a common name and it is stated that they are three persons, just as three men or three persons, as if there were three proper relations by which the person of the Father, the person of the Son, and the person of the Holy Spirit could be understood. And although it is proper to the Father that he has begotten, and proper to the Son that he is begotten, and proper to the Holy Spirit that he proceeds from both, in these individual designations there is understood no separation of nature, but a recognition of persons. So much for the

---

quorum certa pro sui forma esset agnitio. This occurs in the midst of a discussion of stage characters and their masks. The source of this second definition of *persona* has eluded detection until now. Brooke, in "The Speculative Development" p. 37, n. 148, claims to have found William's definition in an anonymous twelfth-century work entitled *De diversitate naturae et personae.* The passage indicated by Brooke is reminiscent of the section of Boethius in which the definition occurs. Both William and the anonymous author of the *De diversitate* seem to rely on Boethius as a common source. The so-called definition of *persona* in the *De diversitate* is, however, a paraphrase of Boethius; it states that the character portrayed by an actor is recognized and identified by his mask. See J. DeGhellinck. "L'histoire de *persona* et d'*hypostasis* dans un écrit anonyme porrétain de XIIe siècle," *Revue néoscolastique de philosophie* 36 (1934) p. 115 for the text.

151. The source of this mode of expression is the *Quicumque* Symbol 15-16. See Par. 46; also compare Aug., *De trin.* 5:8.

name of "person" which the holy Fathers introduced for the sake of the reasoning of faith. It has not seemed unjust to the Church of God in organizing the dogma of the faith that the holy Fathers should have great authority, for they endured great hardships for the faith, even to the shedding of their blood and the death of their bodies.

35. Therefore, I believe in and confess that there is one God in three persons; that is, three persons expressed as distinct in their properties; not merely names, but properties of names, that is, persons, or as the Greeks say, *hypostases,* which is to say subsistences. And the Father never excludes the person of the Son or of the Holy Spirit; nor, conversely do the Son or the Holy Spirit receive the name and person of the Father. The Father is always Father; the Son always Son; and the Holy Spirit always Holy Spirit. Thus, they are one in substance, but distinct in person and name.[152] And this is my faith because it is the Catholic faith concerning the Lord our God, Father, Son, and Holy Spirit.[153] Through the understanding of these things, such as is possible with things of this kind, man proceeds to a knowledge of the Divinity such as is possible. This knowledge continues first, by not doubting with any infidelity what is to be believed; then, by defining without foolhardiness what is to be understood; finally, by adhering faithfully and very devoutly to the truth when it appears.

DEGREES OF KNOWLEDGE

36. Now it is by three degrees of understanding that faith must progress in its ascent to God and the knowledge of God.

---

152. Thus far the paragraph is taken from Pseudo-Jerome, *Ep.* 16 which is actually the *Libellus* of Pelagius, PL 48:489BC. The *Libellus* was known to William as *Ep.* 16 of Jerome. He uses it as a source here and in his *On the Errors of William of Conches,* PL 180:336BC. The *Libellus* was available to the authors of the Middle Ages both as *Ep.* 16 of Jerome and as *Sermo* 236 of Augustine. It can be stated with certainty that William knew the text as a work of Jerome for two reasons. First, the passage in the *Enigma* under discussion differs from the corresponding passage in Augustine, *Sermo* 236 which lacks the reference to the Greeks. Second, in the Er Guil the author identifies his source as Jerome.

153. Compare *De trin.* 1:5; also see the beginning of Par. 24 above.

The first degree is to investigate diligently what it should
believe about the Lord its God. The second involves the way
in which to think of and speak about that which is correctly
believed. The third is already the experience of things in thinking of the Lord in goodness as those think of him who seek
him with a simple heart.[154] The first degree is as easy for the
person making the ascent as belief is easy for the one wishing
to believe and to whom faith has already been given. For, as
the Apostle says, "not all men have faith."[155] The second is
more difficult as it is more remote from the nature of things;
it is for those who, as the same Apostle says, "by custom
have their faculties trained to discern good and evil."[156]
Nevertheless, it may also be presumed by the curious. The
third degree is that of the perfect who with their whole heart,
their whole soul, and their whole mind strive to love the Lord
their God.[157] They already have the first-fruits and the pledge
of the Spirit[158] because they are Sons of God.

   37. The first degree, which is founded on authority, is that
of faith, and it has the form of faith which has been formed
from the credible witness of a proven authority.[159] The
second is that of reason, not of human reason, but of that
which is proper to faith and which has itself the form of
words sound in faith,[160] and in agreement with divine authority in all things. It pertains to this degree not only to think
and speak about God reasonably according to the reasoning
of faith,[161] but to know how that same faith is produced
where it does not exist, how it is nourished and aided where
it does exist, and how it is defended against enemies. Now,
the third degree is that of illumining and beautifying grace

154. Cf. Wisdom 1:1.
155. 2 Thess 3:2.
156. Heb 5:14.
157. Cf. Mt 22:37.
158. Cf. Rom 8:23; 2 Cor 1:22.
159. Compare the *Exposition on the Song of Songs,* Preface 18, CF 6, p. 14
where *forma fidei* is a synonym for the Creed.
160. Cf. 2 Tim 1:13.
161. Rom 12:6. See the section of the introduction on William's sources for a
discussion of *ratio fidei.* This Latin phrase is translated as "reasoning of faith"
throughout the translation.

which puts an end to faith, or rather transforms it beatifical-
ly into love. It conveys a person from faith to vision by
initiating a knowledge which is not that which faith possesses. This knowledge begins to exist with faith during this life
in the man who believes, but concerning it the Apostle says,
"Now I know in part, but then I will know even as I am
known."[162] This is the knowledge which perfect love begins
in this life, and which is to be perfected in the next.[163] But
the knowledge of the present time is a thing of faith, or
rather it is that faith through which God is known, as he can
be known through faith; and he is known to the degree that
he is believed in. This takes its beginning in the first degree of
understanding, has its growth in the second, and is perfected
in the third when in a sense it disappears and there occurs a
transition from the faith of one who believes and hopes to
the knowledge and joy of one who possesses and enjoys, or
begins to possess and enjoy.

38. Now, these two kinds of knowledge differ from one
another as much as God, in what he is in himself, differs from
whatever a man through his humanity can know of God
through thought or discussion. It is evident to all, even to
those who have a slight knowledge of God, that man can
think about God better than he can say anything about him,
although God is far different from anything man can think or
say about him.[164] Nevertheless, this first knowledge concerning God consists in knowing him rationally according to the
reasoning of faith and in thinking of him or speaking about
him. That this is not at all perfect knowledge of the truth is
clearly indicated by the fact that it is often more evident in
many who do not believe as they should than in many more
who are faithful and who, in fact, do believe correctly but are
not able to discern that which they believe. This knowledge,
sometimes passing by the most ardent lovers of the truth,
does not deny itself to many lovers of vanity. Indeed, many
such people know much about God or strive to know much
either simply for the sake of knowing and of satisfying their

162. 1 Cor 13:12.
163. Compare *De trin.* 9:1 for a similar statement and William's source.
164. The same idea is expressed similarly in *De trin.* 7:4.

curiosity; or in order to appear knowledgeable or to be knowledgeable; but in this they seek their own glory and not God's. This is that knowledge of God which the Psalmist says night declares to night;[165] that is, man to man, flesh and blood to flesh and blood, and sometimes the infidel to the infidel. It is far removed from the wisdom and the word which day does not declare, but rather pours forth, to day, or spiritual man to spiritual man, or the Holy Spirit himself through his own actions to the spirit of any holy man; that is, by some hidden inspiration he enters in accompanied by a feeling of God's presence and a savoring of supreme Wisdom. However, since this knowledge is of the greatest necessity for the exercise of piety, if it is treated with piety when it has been entrusted to a person because of his pious endeavors, it should be sought after by all men without exception and embraced with great eagerness. It will not be useless for the growth of faith if it is managed soberly and in accordance with the reasoning of faith. Just as it is very dangerous in the things of God to taste what is lofty, so it is praiseworthy to taste with sobriety.[166] That is, if someone not only in speech or in writing but even in thought considers that he should undertake to investigate every question about the supreme, unchangeable and inscrutable nature, he and every human being should be totally restrained and held back from such an immense and vain presumption. But to investigate these things to the extent that the ability is not denied to man or to the degree that it is forbidden a faithful man to be ignorant of them, the spirit of the man of faith must be helped and exhorted, not discouraged.

39. Just as it is thought no sin to be incapable of knowing what is beyond man concerning the Lord God, our Creator, so, the man who does not apply himself when he can know something, or who neglects to exert sufficient effort to become able when he is not yet able to know, not only is judged before God as guilty of ignorance of God, but is condemned to the punishment he deserves. That is, he who was unwilling to know or act when he was able, when he shall be willing shall not be able. But also, in those things he curiously

165. Cf. Ps 18:3.
166. Cf. Rom 12:3.

pursues to the neglect of God, he is punished in this life; and
in the next he will be thrown into the exterior darkness
(whatever that is) which is read about in the Gospel.[167]
Therefore, once we have embarked upon the path of seeking
God, let us not grow weary, let us not stop. He is faithful
who has promised saying, "Seek and you shall find."[168] And
the Apostle says, "Run so as to obtain the prize."[169] And he
says of himself, "Brothers, I do not think I have obtained it.
But one thing I do, forgetting what is behind and stretching
on to what lies ahead, I press on toward the goal, toward the
prize of the heavenly calling in Christ Jesus, the Lord."[170]
And he added, "As many of us as are perfect, let us be of this
mind."[171] What mind? Namely, that as long as we travel far
from the Lord, walking by faith,[172] we are travellers and have
not reached our destination; and that the perfection of this
life consists in being a vigorous traveller in the way of
faith.[173] However, the arrival belongs to the next life. Therefore, let us proceed piously and humbly on this path on
which we are walking and let us venerate the footsteps of the
Fathers who have gone before. And in the meantime as we
examine the mysteries of this first knowledge of God which
is through faith, let us call upon him who made darkness his
cover,[174] not that he might not be seen but that he might be
sought after more carefully, and to the degree that he would
be sought after more carefully, to be more dearly loved when
he shall have been found. Through his help and his instruction,
let us strive and seek to understand him through faith to the
degree that he grants this for now; later it will be through his
grace that we pass from faith to vision.

DIVINE NAMES

40. Now, the basic elements of the knowledge of God

---

167. Mt 22:13.
168. Lk 11:9.
169. 1Cor 9:24.
170. Phil 3:13-14.
171. Phil 3:15.
172. 2 Cor 5:6-7.
173. For this same imagery of man as traveller see Par. 21.
174. Ps 17:12.

which comes through faith, and by which God is known through faith, are the Divine Names by means of which God is named among men. And harmonious with these is the pattern of words sound in faith.[175] Indeed, the word "names" is derived from *noticia* meaning knowledge.[176] Now, so we may proceed step by step, just as we have already examined above,[177] according to the right order of approaching God, we must first know, concerning the reality to be known, what that is which can only be designated by some name; and secondly, what kind of reality it is or in what manner it exists, so that faith may be in conformity with the thing as it actually is.[178] Now, just as with letters the basic elements are joined together into syllables, the syllables into words, and these, coupled according to the will of the person putting them together, effect some understanding in the heart of the reader, in the same way, the Divine Names, by which God is addressed among men, are joined to one another according to the form of words sound in faith[179] and according to the reasoning of faith, and they produce some understanding of faith in the heart of the believer concerning the hidden things of God. On this account the Apostle Paul said teaching a beloved disciple in the faith about things which he has an obligation to teach, "Having the form of sound words which

175. Cf. 2 Tim 1:13.

176. This etymology is not original with William. While his exact source for this has not yet been determined, the etymology is known to occur in at least two early grammatical works. The first of these is Paul the Deacon's eighth-century epitome of Festus' *De verborum significatu,* itself a work of the late second century. See Wallace M. Lindsay, ed., *Sexti Pompei Festi De verborum significatu quae supersunt cum Pauli epitome* (Leipzig, 1913) p. 179. The etymology is also found in Bern MS 207, Julian of Toledo's *Commentarium in Donatum;* see H. Hagen, ed., *Anecdota Helvetica* (Leipzig, 1870) p. ccv. No material related to this etymology of *nomen* has been found in Donatus himself.

177. See Pars. 36-39 for a discussion of the degrees of our knowledge of God.

178. The Latin for the final clause in this sentence is *ut sicut res est, sic de ipsa fides captetur.* The source for this is Boethius, *De trin.,* PL 64:1250A. Boethius, however, refers the statement to someone else: *sicut optime dictum.* This seems to refer to Cicero, *Tusculanae disputationes* 5:7. William uses this same expression in the *De sacramento altaris,* PL 180:345B where he refers it to Boethius by name. It also appears in *Meditation 12,* CF 3, p. 173.

179. 2 Tim 1:13.

you have heard from me in the faith and have learned in Christ Jesus, guard the good which has been entrusted to you."[180] From this we learn that to guard the deposit of faith and its form, the form of words sound in faith must be especially maintained.

41. Indeed, there is a form of the faith and a form of words sound in faith. The form of the faith concerning the Father, the Son, and Holy Spirit, just as already has often been said, is that the Father is God, the Son is God, and the Holy Spirit is God, and yet there are not three gods, but one God.[181] However, the form of the words sound in faith is a special way of speaking about God according to the very things we have previously set forth. It is a way of speaking based on the authority of Christ the Lord and of the Apostles and apostolic teachers, and which in time past the usage of pious Christians developed concerning the Divine Names and that which is said in the confession of faith about the Father, Son, and Holy Spirit. However, this way of speaking about God has its own discipline supported by the rules and limits of faith so as to teach a manner of speaking about God reasonably according to the reasoning of faith and to prepare men to think about and perceive the ineffable in an ineffable way.[182] Now, we say "according to the reasoning of faith" because this manner of speaking about God has certain special words which are rational but not intelligible except in the reasoning of faith, not however in the reasoning of human understanding. What we said a little earlier—that the Father is God, the Son is God, and the Holy Spirit is God, but that there are not three gods but one God—is understood to some extent according to the reasoning of faith, but not at all according to the reasoning of human understanding.[183] For, in human matters human reason acquires faith for itself,

180. 2 Tim 1:13-14.
181. See the end of Par. 28 above and the beginning of Par. 34. Compare *Quicumque* Symbol 15-16.
182. See Par. 32 above for a similar expression concerning the ineffable character of God.
183. See above in this same paragraph.

but in divine affairs faith comes first and then forms its own
unique reasoning. The most correct way of reasoning is to
conform faith to the object exactly as it is and to adapt the
form of speaking to that faith. However, discourse or inquiry
about God loves the humble and the simple who seek God in
poverty of spirit[184] and who are not driven to this inquiry by
curiosity but are drawn on by piety. It loves to speak not
with rash words or strange words, but with the very words
with which the Word of God manifested himself and the
Father and the Holy Spirit to the world, and with that style
of speech with which men of God have spread faith in the
Trinity through the world. It hates contentions, anger, novelty, arguments and the torments of inane questions. Rather, it
is by experience itself that it instructs those who believe, and
teaches them to attain the reward of contemplation through
the meritorious practice of faith.

42. However, the names, which we have said are the basic
elements of discourse about God, are either the means by
which the Divinity through itself has revealed itself in the
world; that is, the names of Father, and of Son, and of Holy
Spirit; or the means by which it has caused itself to be named
among men, that is, with different considerations of itself
prompting different names.[185] Indeed, in man created in the
image of God there is present a natural longing for knowledge
of God and his own origin. And this follows from the fact
that there is no human mind, whatever its ability to reason
may be, which nature permits to doubt that there is a God,
that he is the Creator of all, and that power and providence
over all things is his possession. Indeed, human piety and
curiosity are, so to speak, by nature involved in a continuous
search to understand in some way what God is. Therefore,
either by understanding the invisible things of God through
those things which have been made,[186] or through the natural
sense of reason, or through the gift of revealing grace, men
have used as many names for God as they have had reflec-

184. Mt 5:3.
185. See the beginning of Par. 40 above.
186. Rom 1:20.

tions about him, such as powerful, wise, wisdom, power, and many other names of this kind. Although even men are very often called by these names, for they are said to be wise or powerful; nevertheless, no one is said to be wisdom or power or other entities of this kind, because no one is wise or powerful in the same way as God. This is because for God being is being wise and being powerful; and he is his wisdom, he is his power.[187] It must be understood thus with truth, with love, and the other names of this sort; that is, the names by which God can be spoken of substantially.

43. Now, there is no uniform system to the Divine Names. Some are spoken of God substantially, some in another way. For, in realities also, everything which exists is either a subject or is in a subject; that is, is either substance or accident. But this is not so in God. For, never is something spoken about God as an accident, but neither is it always spoken of as a substance, for it is also spoken of relatively.[188] In this discussion it must be realized first of all that predicaments of this kind are alien to the nature of faith; that is, substance and accident, and what is called relation, and genus and species, and other similar terms. Truly, these are common, ordinary instruments of reasoning and human skill for discerning common realities. However, for divine realities they are absolutely unworthy and are alien to the form of words sound in faith.[189] Nevertheless, the reasoning of faith, as if humoring human reason,[190] does not entirely despise or reject what is offered it by men, but adopts these things for itself

---

187. See the middle of Par. 50 below. Compare *De trin.* 7:1; the equation of *sapere* and *esse* in God is especially common in *De trin.* 7. William makes this same equation in several places in the *Enigma;* also see Er Guil, PL 180:336B.

188. William's source here is *De trin.* 5:5. These distinctions, *secundum accidens* and *secundum substantiam,* are common in Augustine, for example, *De trin.* 5:3; 5:5; 5:16.

189. Cf 2 Tim 1:13.

190. The phrase "humoring human reason" renders *morem gerens humane rationi.* This is a pre-classical and classical expression. It was used by Ennius, Plautus, Cicero; however, after Cicero it is rare. The expression means *voluntati obtemperare* or *indulgere;* see TLL 6(2):1942 lines 41-82. See an instance of the use of this expression by William's contemporary, Bernard of Clairvaux, in *De consideratione* 3:3:13.

and by adapting each element and conforming it to its own
rules, it in some way subjugates their understanding as a
captive, so to speak, to the service of the faith.[191] This is why
so many names, which in reference to common realities are
names of accidents, are found to be predicated substantially
when transferred to God where the reasoning of faith does
not allow anything spoken of as an accident. For example,
when God is said to be great without quantity and good
without quality, what is understood except that terms of this
kind inasmuch as they are accidents are not admitted, and
yet they are admitted, and inasmuch as they are naturally in
God, as they are nowhere else, they are substantially predicated?   But also, where there is no accident neither is
there a substance. For, that is not a substance nor can it be,
which does not underlie any accidents nor is able to do so. It
is true, indeed, that the supreme simplicity of the divine
nature cannot be the recipient of any accidents, for if it
could receive them it would not be simplicity. That nature
must truly be called simple which does not possess anything
which it can lose (for, that which is unchangeable can seem to
be changeable either by adding something or by taking something away), or which is not constituted of a part possessing,
and a part possessed. And accordingly, that supreme nature is
truly simple because in it quality or quantity are not one
thing and substance another; nor is it through participation
with something other that it is what it is, either powerful, or
wise, or blessed. Therefore, it is better called essence than
substance as will appear more clearly in what follows. And
yet by our very use of language we frequently, and wrongly,
use the name of substance in speaking of God.

44. Still, this name can perhaps be spoken in reference to
God due to another consideration, that he be understood as
subsisting through himself or as that which subsists in all
things which are, as the principle and the cause and the reason of their subsistence. Otherwise, however, it is altogether
improperly said that there is substance in God. Therefore,

191. Cf. 2 Cor 10:5.

when it is necessary to discuss God, the discussion need not always deal with substance, and must never deal with accidents. And even when one speaks relatively, as when the Father is spoken of in relation to the Son, and the Son in relation to the Father, and the Holy Spirit in relation to either or them, it must in no way be understood according to accidents. For, never has the Son approached the eternal and everlasting Father so that he might become Father as if he were not previously, since he always was, or rather, always is Father. And the Son is always consubstantial to the Eternal Father and coeternally from him, and the Holy Spirit exists coeternally from the Father and the Son and is consubstantial to them.

45. But God the Trinity must in no way be thought of according to genus and species; although some who think wrongly about God depict him this way and try to assert that the three persons are three species of one essence.[192] This happens even when the reasoning of faith professes, and the truth proclaims, what cannot in any way be refuted: that the essence is nothing else but the three persons and the three persons are the essence. Thus, God the Trinity should not be thought of in terms of genus and species. But neither should the Trinity be thought of completely in relative terms except according to the measure of faith.[193] Indeed, relation is no more a possession of the one God than of one man. Still, relation is there—the relation of the Father to the Son, of the Son to the Father, of the Holy Spirit to both of these—and it constitutes the Trinity; although beyond every rule of relationships one substance maintains its own very real and very complete unity. Terms of this kind may therefore serve in a discussion about God, since they are not always found to be useless if they are used and controlled in a reasonable manner according to the reasoning of faith. Therefore when a term of this kind is introduced let attention be given not so much to

192. Compare William's criticism of Abelard in his Adv Abl 3 where he accuses Abelard of speaking of the generation of the Son from the Father as one of species from genus.
193. Cf. Rom 12:3.

the term itself as to what the reasoning of faith wishes to make of it. Let us not subject the cause of our faith to reason or the reasoning of men, but rather subject all things to it. Where it is necessary let these terms be of assistance but do not let them become involved more than is necessary. Progress should be made simply in a simple way. Let them speak according to the Gospel who profess to live according to the Gospel.

46. So that we may continue now with our treatment of the Divine Names, we must first carefully observe how these names are understood; that is, the common names as common, but the individual names as individual. Now, those names are said to be common which are predicated of God according to substance, such as power, wisdom, love, God; however, those are individual which are used relatively, such as Father, Son, Holy Spirit. Concerning these especially we must affirm what we already said above:[194] that whatever this supreme, divine Sublimity is called absolutely is predicated substantially, but what is said in reference to relation is said not substantially, but relatively; and that so great is the force of the same substance in the Father and the Son and the Holy Spirit that whatever is said absolutely about each one is to be taken not collectively in the plural, but in the singular. Therefore, all the names which are of this kind are called common. Thus God is said to be the Father, God is said to be the Son, and God is said to be the Holy Spirit; and yet there are not three gods, but one God. The Father is great, the Son is great, and the Holy Spirit is great, but not three are great, but one is great.[195] And one must think thus about power, wisdom, love, truth, and all the names, by means of which, as has been said,[196] the divine majesty is spoken of essentially and substantially.[197] When any of these names is spoken it

194. See the end of Par. 28 and beginning of Par. 29.
195. The previous four sentences occur in *De trin.* 5:8. William uses this same passage in his work on the errors of William of Conches, PL 180:335D-336A. See above in Par. 28 for part of this same passage.
196. See above in this same paragraph.
197. Compare Er Guil, PL 180:336A.

announces not what kind of entity the divine majesty is, but
what it is. But it is clear how individual or singular names are
referred to one another; that is, Father to Son, Son to Father, Father and Son to Holy Spirit, and he to them. Thus, in
this way the names of the supreme essence which are essential and the names of the Trinity by which three are related
to one another both predicate unity and are not silent about
Trinity, each in its own way. The former, in that they are
common to three, demonstrate a Trinity of persons; in that
collectively they are always one they demonstrate the con-
susbstantial unity. However, the latter, in that they are individual and proper to each person, demonstrate the truth of
the Trinity. And these demonstrate unity of substance by the
fact that they are relative and that they indicate by the very
name of the particular quality they express that they are related to one another.

47. Now let us continue with the essence of God and its
names: that is, those names which are called essential from
the essence itself. The origin of these is in that which God
said to his servant Moses who was asking his name, "I am
who am."[98] Thus he said, "You will say to the children of
Israel, 'He who is has sent me to you'."[198] Just as from what
it is to subsist "substance" is spoken of, so from what it is to
be "essence" is spoken of.[199] Now, it has already been said
above in what way "substance" is not suitable to God;[200] although Scripture often improperly uses this name. It is clear
to all how more validly and worthily the name of essence is
applied to God.[201] Indeed, he alone should be said truly to
be, who is unchangeable from eternity; for him, to be is what
he is. And what he is he always is; and just as he is, so he is
always. He does not possess in himself the possibility not to
be what he is, because he does not possess in himself the
possibility to be what he is not. And what he is is not pre-
ceded by a beginning, is not brought to an end by a conclu-

198. Ex 3:14.
199. These definitions occur in *De trin.* 7:4.
200. See the end of Par. 43 above.
201. The first part of this paragraph is based on *De trin.* 7:5.

sion, does not pass through time, is not contained in space, is not changed by age. Nothing is lacking there because everything is in him; nothing is excluded because nothing is outside of him. It is his nature, therefore, always to be able to be what he is; he alone, or almost alone, must be said to be. Thus, it is known most certainly from the Scriptures and must be piously believed that he is Father, he is Son, he is Holy Spirit; that the same one is not Father who is Son, nor is he Holy Spirit who is Father or Son.[202] However, we avoid saying there are three essences in God no less than we avoid saying there are three gods, since in God it is not one thing to be and another to be God, it is the same thing.[203]

48. Therefore, according to the form of words which are sound in faith[204] and the rule established from the reasoning of faith concerning the essential names of God, we say that the essence is the Father, the essence is the Son, the essence is the Holy Spirit and yet there are not three essences, but one essence. However, all these names, which are called essential from "essence," give a certain expression to their source and to the reality of which they are names; just as there are three there and the three are one, so all the names are one and one is all. For, just as God is conceived of by one of these names, so he is conceived of by all; he is not more completely conceived of by all than by one of them. One of these goods which are signified by so many names is as all of them; all are as one. For, in God to be able is to will, to be wise, to know, and all the other attributes which, as has been said, are predicated of God essentially and absolutely.[205] For, God has no potential in any other way, nor does he will in any other way, nor is he wise in any other way, nor does he know in any other way, for he is not this in one way and that in another. He simply is what he is. Nor should it be thought

202. Almost the same sentence occurs at the end of Par. 32 above. See note 147.

203. Compare the beginning of Par. 33 above. For this sentence compare *De trin.* 7:4, "It is no more proper to speak of three essences than three gods." Also, *De trin.* 7:1, "For God it is not one thing to be and another to be God."

204. Cf 2 Tim 1:13.

205. See the end of Par. 42.

or believed that the supreme good is a composite from all these goods, because no less is the supreme good in each than in all, but it is completely in each and it is one in all.[206] Otherwise, our God would not be simple but multiple. In addition, however, all these attributes are at the same time present in the Trinity of single persons in such a way that just as all of these are one in God, so each person in the Trinity is all of these.

49. Now, sometimes the Father is called Power, the Son Wisdom, and the Holy Spirit Goodness;[207] but, when this is said the Catholic mind ought to observe carefully and vigilantly that in this way some of those attributes which are common to the three persons, are sometimes ascribed to a single person.[208] This is done in order to draw together and to prepare for the human intelligence an explanation of the harmony of divine cooperation. But just as there is a single operation of the three persons of the Trinity, so also in all of these, inasmuch as it is in God, a single, similar operation must be understood, although the same operation does not reach a creature as it sets out from God. For, just as God is not powerful in one way, wise in another, and good in another; so, inasmuch as it is in him, those things which concern power are not different from those which concern wisdom or

206. See the first half of Par. 32.

207. See these attributes in Hugh of St Victor, *De sacramentis* 1:2.

208. See William's *Disputation against Abelard* 2, PL 180:250AB, where he criticizes Abelard's attribution of *potentia, sapientia,* and *charitas* or *benignitas* to the Father, Son, and Holy Spirit respectively. William finds fault with Abelard's manner of attributing these names to the Trinity. Abelard says they are spoken of God in a descriptive way; see *Disputation* 2, PL 180:250B. William attacks this position and says in the same section, PL 180:250B, that the names are spoken of God traditionally as a profession of faith, not as a description of the Divinity; if God could be described he could also be circumscribed. The same issue of the names of God forms the core of William's difficulties with William of Conches whose *Summa philosophiae* he read when a copy was brought to Signy by an entering novice. William of St Thierry quotes from the *Summa* in his Er Guil, PL 180:333C; he sees William of Conches' position as a threat to the unity of the Trinity and responds with several passages from Augustine and one from Pseudo-Jerome; nine of these passages occur again in the *Enigma.* Finally, William appeals to *ratio fidei* to defend a proper understanding of the names attributed to God.

goodness; although, in creatures who are different from one another the effects of that operation, while similar, will appear dissimilar. But although the Divine Names of this kind suit the three persons in the Trinity equally because of their unity of nature, as was said above, certain of them seem to be ascribed more commonly and more frequently to certain persons in the Trinity. This is just as we said before; namely, power is ascribed to the Father, wisdom to the Son, and goodness to the Holy Spirit. This is done for distinction of persons that they may be distinguished, not that they may be separated. Except for relative names by which the Father, Son, and Holy Spirit are spoken of in relation to one another and which are individual and proper to a single person, by whatever name one of the persons is designated, they are all likewise designated, because they are all one in that by which they are named.

50. But the Son is spoken of not only as God who is wisdom, but also as the wisdom of God; and the Holy Spirit as the goodness of God, and this must, indeed, be understood according to the reasoning of faith.[209] Truly, the Son is the wisdom of the Father, not the wisdom by which the Father is wise, since he is all-wise in himself and is supreme wisdom, but in the Son is the wisdom of the Father for this reason: he is wisdom and this existence is his from the Father from whom he possesses all that he is. Indeed, the Son is from the Father, wisdom from wisdom, one wisdom with the Father; in the same way he is substance or rather essence from essence, one essence with the Father. Now, if the Son is called the wisdom of the Father as if to imply that the Father is wise through that wisdom, then the Son would be not so much the Son as a quality of the Father. But in addition, since for God to be wise is the same as to be,[210] and the wisdom of the Father is one essence with the Father, if the Son were the wisdom of the Father in such a way that only by that wisdom

209. Par. 50 is drawn from *De trin.* 77:1. Some of this same material from Augustine occurs in William's Exp Rm 6.
210. See the end of Par. 42 above and the note on the equation of *sapere* and *esse* in God.

which is the Son could the Father be wise, then the Son would be not so much the Son of the Father as his essence, and then in agreement with Sabellius the Son would be who the Father is. The goodness which the Holy Spirit is said to be must be understood in the same way. But, lest through the mention of the individual attributes by which the Father is called Power, the Son Wisdom, and the Holy Spirit Goodness the persons be understood as separable in any way, the reasoning of faith is immediately at hand by which the same individual names of each person can also be spoken of the three together; so that not only is the Father called Power, but the Son and Holy Spirit are also; not only is the Son called Wisdom, but the Father and the Holy Spirit also; not only is the Holy Spirit called Goodness, but the Father and the Son also. And when, concerning the providence of creation, power is predicated of the Father, wisdom of the Son, and goodness of the Holy Spirit, these names for God must be understood in no other way than that there is predicated the operation of the one Divinity who is omnipotent, wise, and all-good, so that in these names which are spoken, the cooperation of the Trinity can be understood.

51. When Holy Scripture speaks of this cooperation in such a way that either in deeds or in words or in names of this kind it assigns something to the individual persons which seems suitable for each of them, do not let the Catholic faith be troubled, but let it be taught that through the individuality of either the word or the deed, the truth of the Trinity is made known to us. And do not let the understanding divide what the ear distinguishes. In this way, certain things are expressed under the name of the Father or of the Son or of the Holy Spirit, so that the confession of those who believe in the Trinity might not be in error. Although the Trinity is indivisible, the Trinity could never be understood if it were always spoken of indivisibly. Fortunately, therefore, the difficulty of speaking draws our hearts to understanding and through our weakness the heavenly teaching helps us so that true unity and trinity can to some extent be understood by our minds even if it cannot likewise be expressed by our

mouths. Indeed, neither singularity nor diversity is to be thought of in the Deity of the Father, the Son, and the Holy Spirit.[211] This might be said of the essential names of God about which all we are saying is nothing, for whatever can be said of God is nothing really, because that which is ineffable cannot be explained with words. Words fail; the understanding is in darkness. Still, since we are commanded always to seek the face of the Lord,[212] and since what is ordered by God contains a promise we must not despair; the understanding must be set free and the attempt to verbalize encouraged to the utmost. And when human ability fails, the nature of God must be honored in silence.

52. Now it must be realized that that supreme majesty which is called God is powerful, wise, and good, and the other attributes of this kind by which he is spoken of essentially and absolutely. And all these names can be said of creation also. Indeed, God, who is in himself who he is, in relation to creation is the God of all things which are, inasmuch as he is creator, ruler, and Lord of all things which are not what he himself is. He who has the power within himself to be what he is, in relation to all creation is not only powerful in all respects, but is even omnipotent. And for God, for whom to know himself and to be wise is to be, his knowledge or wisdom is not one thing in regard to himself, and another in regard to creation. And he is in himself not so much good, as that essential good by which anything is good which is in any way good. In relation to all his creation he is the supreme good, and is so very good that nothing better can be thought of; and he is the source of well-being for whatever is prosperous.

53. This is the same sense in which one must understand almost all the Divine Names by which God is spoken of absolutely, namely, that in reference to creation he is also spoken of with those names by which he is spoken of in reference to himself. This is done not so much relatively, as though it

211. Par. 51 to this point is borrowed from Leo the Great, *Sermo* 76:2.
212. 1 Chron 16:11. See above, note 114.

were from creation that he possessed what he is said to be in relation to creation, as by means of a conferral, if such a thing can be said, that is, by giving to creation that it be that in relation to which God is spoken of. Hence God is said to be great in relation to creation in comparison with that creation; he is great in himself without any comparison. He is just in relation to creation because he disposes all things justly; yet, in that which he is, inasmuch as he is, he is just; he is most just in himself. And so forth in this manner. Now, whatever is understood by God's names of this kind with reference to creation God is in such a way that—as has been said concerning his essential names—he exists not as if he had his being from these his parts, for he is not this and this separately, he is not this or this singly. He is not in one part what he is not in another. But he is what he is; and he is all these, and none of these are accidents because he does not obtain all these from another, but possesses them essentially. He possesses nothing in himself except that which he is. And just as all these things are in him not as one thing and another, but are simply one; so they are in him not in one way and another, but simply and in a single modality that is without any modality.

54. There are certainly some of these names which when said of God seem to present the appearance of relative accidents, as when God is called Creator, Lord, or Principle[213] in reference to creation. But they must not be interpreted at all in this way since it is the nature of all accidents to modify their subject and therefore none of them can inhere in an unchangeable substance. For God, to be eternal is to be Creator or Lord or Principle, although that creation has not always existed of which he is Creator, Lord, and Principle. This is difficult to understand. Men have tried to express themselves in some way concerning the ineffable, and, unable to do this except with words, they have said that God is

213. See Jn 8:25; William calls God *principium*. It was a common patristic interpretation of this verse in John that Christ was speaking of himself as *principium*. See Ambrose, *De fide* 3:7, PL 16:600A; Augustine, *In Johannis evang.* 38:11; *De trin.* 5:13.

Creator, Lord, and Principle. In a situation where no words are adequate they have not found words more suitable than these for saying these things which must be said in this way. Although these words are clear and certainly true because God has created all things and is the Lord and Principle of all; nevertheless, it is difficult to understand how an accident is not implied when, as has been said, the name of temporal creation is joined in time to the Eternal. But every accident, by being added or taken away, as has been said, necessarily modifies its subject and this is incompatible with an unchangeable God. But when these things and similar things are said of God they must be attributed to that unchangeable substance in such a way that they are said in some way proper to the Divinity but relative to creation. This must be in such a way that although at some point in time a name of this kind begins to be said of God, it is not understood to inhere in the very substance of God which is thus spoken of, but in that creature in reference to which the name is used.[214] Consequently, when we take refuge in God,[215] no change is made in him or in his nature; however, we are changed since we who were worse are made better. So also, when he begins to be our Father he is not changed; rather, we are regenerated and made sons of God through the grace of him who gave us the power to become sons of God.[216] And when we are made sons of God our substance truly is transformed for the better, but he begins to be our Father without any change of his substance. And when some just man begins to be made a friend of God, he is changed; but heaven forbid that God be changed who loves no one in time as if with a new love which was not in him before, and who loved us before the foundation of the world,[217] and for whom past events have not passed away and future events have already taken place. Therefore, whatever name God begins to be called in time

214. The ideas expressed in this sentence and the remainder of Par. 54 are derived from *De trin.* 5:16.
215. Cf. Ps 89:1.
216. Cf. Jn 1:12.
217. Cf. Jn 17:24.

which he was not called before is clearly spoken relatively. But this is not as an accident of God as if something could inhere in him, but plainly as an accident of that in relation to which the name begins to be spoken. When divine realities are spoken of in this way they are not at all spoken of in a way proper to them, but in a way in which what is said can be somehow grasped by the human heart.

55. Therefore, when words are used to treat of God, the sense of the words must be fitted to the realities and not vice versa. Every use of human reasoning expressed in words ought to be only an investigation of truth; and wherever truth presents itself reason ceases to be reason any longer if it does not immediately abandon its concern for words and assent to the truth. Indeed, nothing is more obviously true than that no creature or certainly nothing from a creature inheres as an accident in the unchangeable God. In God the Creator of all things, in whom is all time and whatever is temporal, there is eternity and life; and whatever is future to a given time is already completely present to God from eternity. At no time does a creature created in time cause God to begin to be Creator at some time or other, as if he were not Creator before; although God can begin to be called Creator at any time. But the Creator creating a creature does so without time so that, what did not exist, does exist in its own time. And this act of creation does not so much inhere as an accident in God as God inheres in it as an accident, if it is proper to say this. That substance in which subsists whatever exists can in no way be called an accident, but words fail for saying something which can in any way be understood concerning realities of this kind.

56. Thus, in this way the Divine Names which refer to creation must be understood relatively; although they refer to temporal and mutable creation, they are none the less names of the eternal, unchangeable essence, and must be understood in their own way. Since in God, in whom what has been made is life[218] and in whom whatever is is God,

218. See Jn 1:3. *De trin.* 44:1 contains this same idea that whatever has been made is life in God.

from eternity there is present the principal essence of everything which is temporal; every exterior creation is only an
image of that supreme exemplar and some kind of likeness of
interior truth, not an accident inhering in him, but proceed-
ing from him as a natural source and causal reason in accordance with the order of providence. Although for God who
knows everything being is knowing, every exterior creature is
not therefore known by him because it exists, but exists
because it is known by him.[219] And a creature which is in any
way mortal in itself, to the degree that it is changeable, is life
in the unchangeable Word. For God, to know himself is to be
what he is; he does not know himself in one way and a
creature in another. For, the Creator without time knows
time; the Arranger of all things which are changeable is without change in himself. Those things which exist in any way in
themselves all are life in him. But whatever is life in eternity
does not begin to live at some time nor can it die.

57. Therefore, whatever that creature is, whether living or
not, whether intelligent or not, it is life in God—and this
every creature is—and in some way or other it changes in
itself or is corrupted, it begins and it comes to an end. Its
first and principal essence and the truth of its existence,
which is in God and is God, neither changes nor is corrupted.
God's supreme wisdom unchangeably orders all changeable
things just as he unchangeably creates all that is changeable.
Whatever is more similar to its principle is truer, but it is less
true if it is less similar to its principle. In this way, therefore,
according to the reasoning and form of faith, the name of
Creator, which refers to a creature, is essential to God because he is the principal essence of every creature; and the
name of creature is relative to the Creator in so far as a
creature has its existence from God. Whatever we have said
on this matter is meant to make this point: that although the
names of a creature are spoken in reference to the Creator in
a relative way; nevertheless, the names of the Creator are
understood not as accidents relative to a creature, but as

219. This idea is found in *De trin.* 6:10.

signifying that the principle essence of a creature is in God. This is why according to the rule of all the essential names in God, such names are spoken when the Father is called Creator, and the Son Creator, and the Holy Spirit Creator, and yet there are not three creators but one Creator. The same must be understood of the names of Lord or of Principle, and for the other names by which God is spoken of in relation to creation. Now, since we have in this way classified these names by which God is spoken of in relation to creation with those names by which he is spoken of essentially and with reference to himself, let us pass on to the relative names by which Father, Son, and Holy Spirit are spoken of relatively with reference to one another in the Trinity which is God. But first it must be said that just as essence contains unity, so relation predicates Trinity.

58. Regardless of how little is a man's share of human reason he cannot err in the faith of that unity of which the Lord says, "I and the Father are one";[220] nor can he fail to possess the judgment common to all men concerning that unity; namely, that the Lord God is one God.[221] From the time that our Lord Jesus Christ shone upon the world, not only was the world, or man, ashamed to worship the works of his hands, but the worship of many gods and demons almost fled from the whole world. And in the worship of one God all agreed, not only Jew and Christian, but even pagan and barbarian. At no time did anyone, neither a Christian or Jewish heretic nor a philosopher of the Gentiles, dare openly oppose this belief about God which was held by all. Therefore, even faith in the Trinity, with the scandal of the cross,[222] which long ago from the time of the patriarchs and the prophets had already begun to be revealed to some men in the world, and after that in times of grace came to be preached by all, has become a sign which is contradicted by many,[223] as if it were a sign of the worship of three gods and a reproach to the Crucified.

220. Jn 10:30.
221. Cf. Deut 6:4.
222. Cf. 1 Cor 1:23.
223. Cf. Lk 2:34.

59. I will pass over those who are outside the fold, for sometimes there are faithful within the Church who, when they do not understand what is taught, say, "Why preach the Trinity to us?"[224] Only one God, whoever he is and whatever his nature, should be preached and worshipped." But whoever says this is in error and contradicts the grace of God. "No one has ever seen God, but the only-begotten Son who is in the bosom of the Father has made him known."[225] For this he came into the world; he did this so that he might reveal God the Trinity.[226] Nowhere in this life is the Divinity better grasped by the human understanding than in that by which it is better understood to be incomprehensible: that is, in the preaching of the Trinity.[227] Now, "the Word was made flesh and dwelt among us"[228] so that, just as the Lord Jesus Christ said in his prayer to the Father,[229] he himself might reveal the name of the Father to men and might pour forth the love of God into our hearts through the Holy Spirit whom he has given us.[230] Indeed, this is the enigma of faith whereby,[231] as has often been said already, we say that God is the Father, and God is the Son, and God is the Holy Spirit, and yet there are not three gods but one God.[232] This mystery is terrifying to the impious; it frightens them and causes them to flee from the face of the Lord. It is soothing to the pious; it stirs them up and urges them on to seek his face always.[233]

60. Thus, whoever investigates any concept of the Trinity

---

224. The Latin for this sentence, *Ut quid nobis predicatio Trinitatis?* , parallels Mt 26:8: *Ut quid perditio haec?* This use of *ut quid* to mean "why" is rare.

225. Jn 1:18.

226. Cf. Jn 18:37.

227. William expresses this same idea in *Meditation* 7:7, CF 3, p. 137; see note 24 on that passage. Caution must be had in too quickly associating William's thought here with that of Pseudo-Dionysius. The same idea is found in Hilary, *De trin.* 2:7.

228. Jn 1:14.

229. Cf. Jn 17:6.

230. Cf. Rom 5:5.

231. This is the only occurence of "enigma of faith" in the treatise.

232. This expression, based on *Quicumque* Symbol 15-16, is found several times in the *Enigma,* e.g., the end of Par 28.

233. Cf. 1 Chron 16:11. See above, note 114.

or of divine affairs through verbal images enters into the
labyrinth of divine relations. Such a man should not be one
who scrutinizes God's majesty—he will surely be overwhelm-
ed by his glory[234]—but a man poor in spirit[235] to whom
mercy is always close by. He ought to know that the order of
discussion of human affairs is one thing and that all words
necessary for the expression of those affairs have been found;
but the order of discussion of divine affairs is another thing
and for their expression no words are by any means suitable.
In the former, with the first attempt to learn, the meaning of
the words must be sought through which one can arrive at
the meaning of the reality. On the contrary, in the latter, one
must first of all seek some understanding and sense of the
reality, not so much through the efforts of any learning as
through a pious faith and a fervent love. Then immediately,
the meaning of the words by which the reality is discussed
will present itself to the one who is making progress. For
example, a man inquiring about the relationships in God will
first receive those names or individual words proper to each
of the persons and relative to one another: the Father who
begets, the Son who is begotten, and the Holy Spirit who
proceeds. These names must be received by us as certain
divine instruments for discovering God which have been
transmitted to us by God through men of God who were
filled with God. Nevertheless, these names express very inade-
quately a notion of the realities of which they are signs. As
long as these words help us to increase our knowledge of
God, inasmuch as words can help us, we should respect them
and embrace them. But when these words fail, as words do,
they must be transcended with the grace and blessing of him
whom they name. For when one speaks of the Father as
begetting, the Son as begotten, and the Holy Spirit as pro-
ceeding from both, these are words or names full of divine
truth. But since they also carry a meaning applicable to
human affairs they raise us but little from the earthly and the

234. Cf. Prov 25:27.
235. Cf. Mt 5:3.

human unless, when these words are spoken externally, the realities of faith are thought of internally; namely, in generation and birth and procession nothing is thought of as active, nothing passive, nothing temporal, nothing local, nothing different nor separable, only the one same God.

61. In the Trinity, one is from the other; for one it is a birth, for another a procession: eternal being from eternal being; the coeternity of three. The coming of one from the other is either an eternal birth or an eternal procession. Although the Son is begotten in birth by the Father, and the Holy Spirit proceeds from the Father and the Son, in no way does one withdraw from the other. For, eternally and without change the Father is in the Son, the Son is in the Father, the Holy Spirit is in the Father and the Son, and they are in him in accordance with the truth of the one divine essence. And the Son is from the Father, and the Holy Spirit is from the Father and the Son in accordance with the truth of the the Trinity and of the singularity of persons. Here it is the Trinity itself which is unity and unity which is Trinity. One person of this supreme Trinity is not something less than the whole Trinity; the whole Trinity is not greater than one person in it. The Father did not diminish himself that he might have a Son; rather, he begot from himself another self so that he remains complete in himself, and is as much in the Son as in himself. Likewise, the Son is complete from one who is complete; he is as much in the Father as from the Father. He is always in the Father, always from the Father. He does not lessen him by his birth nor increase him by clinging to him.[236] And just as the Son is from the Father and with the Father, so the Holy Spirit is from both and with both, with this difference: the Son is from the Father through birth; the Holy Spirit is from the Father and the Son through procession. Now, for the Son to be from the Father and to be that which he is, is always to be born; likewise, for the Holy Spirit to be from the Father and from the Son and to be that which they are, is an eternal procession from both.

236. These four sentences are taken from Augustine Ep 170:5. William uses this same passage from Augustine almost verbatim in his Exp Rm 6.

62. Therefore, with this modality God the Trinity must be preached, if there is, in fact, any modality in him by whom and from whom all modality exists. And the persons possess themselves, the one in relation to the other, if there is, in fact, any possession there where God possesses nothing except what he is. And these are the realities which, in order to be understood by men, must be offered to them clothed with the name of Trinity or of three persons or of mutual relationships with one another, in order that men might in some way understand what is almost ineffably preached about God. Indeed, the understanding of divine realities, of which these names are seen to be signs, is not so much given to us through these names, as rather we are informed and nourished by this form of words, sound in faith,[237] in order to understand what we desire about God.

63. Therefore, in order to continue now with what we have begun concerning the relative names: three persons are spoken of relatively in relation to one another, but outside the normal order of relationships because they do not involve any accidents. They are spoken of relatively; that is, the Father in relation to the Son, and the Son in relation to the Father. And this is in no way understood in God as involving an accident. Indeed, for the Father to be called Father and the Son to be called Son is an eternal, unchangeable reality for them. For, the Father is always the Father, and the Son is always the Son. And "always" does not refer to the point from which the Son was born, or to the fact that the Father never ceases to be Father and the Son never ceases to be Son; but rather "always" is used because the Son is always born and the Father at no time begins to be Father nor does the Son begin to be Son. For, if they began at some time, or ceased, this would all involve an accident.[238] Nevertheless, one speaks relatively not only of the Father in relation to the Son and the Son in relation to the Father, and also of the Holy Spirit in relation to Father and Son, and of them in relation to him inasmuch as he is their Spirit and proceeds

237. Cf. 2 Tim 1:13.
238. The first half of this paragraph is taken from *De trin.* 5:5.

from them and they send him forth. It is necessary here to
discuss this more fully, although we have already touched
upon it briefly above. And let everyone judge who can judge
concerning matters of this kind, how what we are saying is
contrary to all reason and the usage of all relative terms.

64. Every essence which is spoken of relatively is also something in itself exclusive of its relation, just as a master is a
man, and a beast of burden is a horse. For, "man" and
"horse" are spoken of absolutely, and arc essences; "master"
and "beast of burden" are spoken of relatively, in relation to
something. If man and horse were not substances of some
kind they could not have the relative names of master and
beast of burden. And therefore, if Father is not something
which can be spoken of absolutely, and likewise son, they are
certainly not something which can be spoken of relatively, in
relation to one another.[239] But when a man who is master
and a man who is slave are spoken of in relation to one
another, there are two men. But, God the Father and God
the Son are not two gods, but one God. Nevertheless, since
the Father is not the Son and the Son is not the Father, and
the Holy Spirit, who is also called the gift of God, is neither
the Father nor the Son, they are indeed really three. And
consequently it is said in the plural, "I and the Father are
one."[240] He did not say "is one," as the Sabellians say; but
"are one." Thus, when there is a question about the Father
and the Son and the Holy Spirit as to what they are, who
they are, whether they are three persons or three things, what
terminology will we use except the relative names by which
they are related to one another? Now, since men have no
names for these three, whether proper or common, with the
exception of the relative names, pious faith understands that
this is not without reason, but understanding that that which
is being considered is ineffable, it is instructed more in the
knowledge of God by its knowledge of human ignorance.
Now, in fact, they are common names when one speaks

239. The paragraph down to here is based on *De trin.* 7:1.
240. Jn 10:30; this and the following sentence are from *De trin.* 5:9.

about "three men"; proper names, when one speaks about Abraham, Isaac and Jacob.[241]

65. Now, here there is nothing other than the nature or essence of the supreme good, which, indeed, if it is supreme, is not three, but one. And its name is God which is the name of only one, for God is only one. Indeed, this is the "one" of which the Lord said, "I and the Father are one."[242] But that whole and divine "one" is in no way composed of different elements, because it is not made up of parts nor can it be broken down into parts. Although in God there is trinity which is unity and unity which is trinity; nevertheless, in no way does the name of unity here signify under the name of Trinity some sort of numerical union of triplicity,[243] but the inseparable simplicity of the divine essence. On account of this, it is in no way proper that the three persons which are spoken of in the inseparable Trinity be spoken of as separable in any way from one another. This is no more proper than to say this of the Trinity itself. For the Trinity should not be called inseparable if the three persons can in any way be separated. However, even if the three persons cannot be spoken of at the same time; nevertheless, they should be conceived of at the same time. For, truly, that is said to be inseparable which in no way admits separation. If anyone

241. William uses these three men as examples just as Augustine had done in *De trin.* 7:4.

242. Jn 10:30.

243. The English "triplicity" translates *triplicitas.* William uses this same word in Par. 76. See Peter Lombard, *Sententiarum liber* 3:19 for the same rejection of triplicity in the Trinity. Earlier uses of *triplicitas* are difficult to find. Lewis and Short, *A Latin Dictionary,* does not include the word. The TLL is not complete far enough to treat it. Forcellini, *Lexicon totius Latinitatis* 4:2 (Patavia, 1887) p. 805 gives only one example of the use of the word, an inscription referring to the Trinity: *triplicitas simplex simplicitasque triplex.* This lone example is likewise reported in other standard lexical works. The inscription is included by de Rossi in *Inscriptiones christianae urbis Romae* (Rome, 1888) Vol. 2, p. 109. This inscription is the only instance of *triplicitas* I have found where the word is accepted as suitable for reference to the Trinity. William and Peter Lombard both reject it. Also, Thomas Aquinas in *Summa theologiae* PI, 31:1 *ad* 3 rejects the word: *non est in Deo triplicitas sed trinitas.* Aquinas makes a reference to Boethius' *De arithmetica* for the word; the Leonine edition of *Summa* (Rome, 1888) Vol. 4, p. 343 gives the location as *De arith.* 1:23, but this does not seem to be accurate.

thinks that the three persons in the Trinity can be separated, the Trinity must not be spoken of as separable, but the unity. Indeed, Trinity consists in the persons unity, in the nature. The nature of the Trinity which alone is everywhere complete, just as it possesses its own being which is both unique and complete, cannot admit a separation of persons. In fact, the persons in the Trinity are named singly, but the Trinity wished to show itself inseparable in persons with the result that there is no name by which any one person can be called in such a way that it is not appropriate to the three in the unity of nature;[244] as for example, when one says powerful, wise, good and other names of this kind. The Trinity's desire to show itself inseparable in persons also results in its demonstrating by its singular name that one person is related to another; namely, when one says Father, Son, and Holy Spirit. For, with relative names, one person is not spoken of singly in such a way that he is not related to another by his very name.[245] Indeed, with a relative name, one person is spoken of singly in reference to himself such that he is not spoken of absolutely. For this reason, the very relation inherent in the name of the person forbids his being separated; for, when the name designates the persons, at the same time it also links them together. For, when Father is said, likewise is understood the Son of whom he is the Father. When Son is said, also is understood the Father whose Son he is. When the Holy Spirit is called the gift, then just as the Son is called the Word in reference to a speaker, so he is inseparably related as a gift to the giver.

66. In respect to the relative names, it is necessary to know that while the names of Father, Son, and Holy Spirit are names which are proper to the persons, with one name for each of them, there are also certain operations proper to each of them; namely, to the Father in that he has begotten; to the Son in that has been begotten; to the Holy Spirit in that he proceeds from both; and there are other things similar to

244. A sentence very similar to this occurs in William's *On the Errors of William of Conches,* PL 180:336C where he attributes it to Augustine.
245. This sentence is paralleled by one in Er Guil, PL 180:336D.

these. However, in these proper operations there is no separation of that nature, but a recognition of persons. For, the three persons are spoken of singly so that they can be known, not so that they can be separated. Just as there is no separation in the persons, so no confusion of persons can be present among them. Nor, I say, should anyone dare say that they are separable in any way, since neither can he find nor should he imagine any of the persons existing or operating before the other, after the other, or without the other. Where there can thus be no separation of operation, an unchangeable unity of nature remains. For example, the whole Trinity made that form which the Only-begotten assumed.[246] Although it was made by the whole Trinity, it is certain that it belongs only to the person of the Son. Although the operation belongs to the whole Trinity, the reception of the form does not. Indeed, the propriety of persons—that he is not the Father who is the Son, nor is he the Holy Spirit who is Father or Son—shows that something has been done by the Father and the Son, which, however, has been received only by the Son. In a similar way must be understood the voice of the Father at the baptism saying, "This is my beloved Son";[247] likewise, the dove and the fire in the appearance of which the Holy Spirit was seen to appear over the Lord and over the Apostles.[248] No example of this reality can be found in creation, since with the exception of the Trinity which is the Lord God by nature, there is no nature which can possess in itself three inseparable persons.

67. Thus, those two predications, essential and relative, concerning God the Father, Son, and Holy Spirit seem to be self-contradictory since the one involves those things which are absolute, and preserves unity everywhere; the other concerns that by which they are related to one another, and preaches the Trinity. Nevertheless, they are more in agreement about this and with love embrace one another as friends in the unity of that peace which surpasses all under-

---

246. This idea is reminiscent of passages in *De trin.* 1:4 and 2:10.
247. Mt 3:17.
248. Mt 3:16; Acts 2:1-4.

standing,[249] since essential predication says there is one God
and does not deny there are three persons; and relative predication says the three persons possess a relationship to one
another, but completely denies that three gods are being
spoken of. And so, continually each one without injury to
the other predicates what belongs to it in such a way that it
neither forsakes what belongs to it nor disturbs in any way
what belongs to the other. And from both of these is established what is proper to the Catholic faith; namely, the reasoning of the faith predicating that unity which is the Trinity, that Trinity which is unity: one God.

68. However, there are other relative names by which God
is spoken of relatively, such as when God the Father, the
principle of divinity, is called the principle in relation to the
Son who is from him; and likewise with the Son in relation to
the Holy Spirit who is from them. Now, the Father and the
Son, but chiefly the Father, are the one principle of the Holy
Spirit,[250] since the Son receives this principle by being born
from the Father so that with the Father he is the one principle of the Holy Spirit. To be sure, when the Father is said
to be the principle chiefly, there must be understood neither
precedence in time, nor superiority or level of dignity, nor
greater or lesser majesty; on the contrary, there is signified
who is from whom, or who is related to whom, or what is
related to what, in that nature of the consubstantial Trinity.
For, the Father derives his origin from no one and is the
origin of divinity.[251] But from him the Son has his origin
which he received by being born from him, so that by his
essential nature the Son is one with the Father. Also, from
the Father and from the Son, but principally, as said before,
from the Father, the Holy Spirit has his being, who by pro-
ceeding from both, has in common with both that he is what
they are. Also, the Son is relatively spoken of as the Word of

249. Cf. Phil 4:7.
250. Compare *De trin.* 15:17.
251. Compare Augustine, Sermo 71:26: "from the Father is the origin of the
operations and from him is the existence of the co-operating persons, for the Son
is born of him, and the Holy Spirit proceeds principally from him."

the Father who speaks, and the Holy Spirit is spoken of as the gift of God who gives. Just as when Father and Son are spoken of, one must not think of a derived succession between the begetter and the begotten, but rather of a mystery of eternal birth; likewise, when the Word of God is mentioned one must not conceive of a word which is uttered,[252] but rather of one that is consubstantial with the speaker and coeternal with him. Likewise, when the Holy Spirit is called the gift of the Father and the Son there is to be no thought of the subordination of that which is given and the superiority of those who are giving, but rather concord between the gift and the givers.[253] For, the mode of that relation is unique, so that, although the relations in the Trinity seem unequal, as for instance, the relations of Father to Son, of speaker to Word, of gift to giver; nevertheless, there is here a supreme equality, since they are one: both the one who is from the other, and the one who is from the two, and the two from whom the one is.

69. Although none of the persons is found to be first or middle or last by those who have correct knowledge of God and by those who think piously about that unity of which the Lord says, "I and the Father are one";[254] nevertheless, it is necessary that in the Trinity three be spoken of distinctly, and also it is necessary that these be mentioned in their order so that it will be intelligible who is from whom. In the first position is placed the Father who has begotten; in the second the Son who is begotten; in the third the Holy Spirit who proceeds from both. This order must also be observed most prudently in the operation of the divinity or the cooperation of the Trinity which seems to be intimately con-

---

252. The phrase "a word which is uttered" attempts to translate *verbum prolativum*. The distinction William makes is that the Word is not uttered or spoken by the Father so as to pass from him. The Word is spoken but remains with the Father. This distinction is found in *De trin.* 7:1. William uses this section of Augustine in his Er Guil, PL 180:337D and attributes it to its author.

253. The latter part of the sentence dealing with the Holy Spirit is borrowed from *De trin.* 15:19. The English "subordination" translates *conditio*. This is a post-classical use of the word.

254. Jn 10:30.

nected with the relation of the three persons; as is the case, for example, in that which the Apostle says, "From whom, through whom, and in whom are all things: to him be glory for ever. Amen."[255] Although in this quotation all things seem to be mentioned as created by the Father through the Son in the Holy Sprit;[256] nevertheless, in the different attributions indicated by the prepositions, there must be understood no diversity of operation, but the simple cooperation of the Trinity. For, all things are equally from the Father and from the Son and from the Holy Spirit as from the nature which is the creator of all; equally through the Father and through the Son and through the Holy Spirit as through God the maker of all; equally in the Father and in the Son and in the Holy Spirit as in God who contains all things. Certainly, in this kind of placement of the three persons or in such attributions as are indicated by the prepositions there is only to be understood an indication of a personal Trinity; in such a way, however, that everything is brought together for understanding in the Trinity the truth of divine unity. The Apostle immediately adds: "to him,"[257] not "to them." Nevertheless, all things are distributed among the persons when all things are said to be from the Father from whom especially every creature exists, and through the Word by whom the Father has spoken and by whom all things were made,[258] and in the Holy Spirit who is the goodness of the Father and the Son, containing all things. And they are said to cooperate whose operation is one just as their essence is one. They are said to cooperate because they are three; and their operation is one because they are one. And consequently the Lord says in the Gospel, "The Son can do nothing of his own accord, but only what he sees the Father doing. For, the Father loves the Son and shows him all that he does."[259]

255. Rom 11:36.
256. Augustine interprets this formula in the same way as William in *De trin.* 1:6: from whom (Father), through whom (Son), and in whom (Holy Spirit).
257. Rom 11:36.
258. Jn 1:3.
259. Jn 5:19-20.

For the Son, to see the Father is to be what the Father is, to see the Father working is to cooperate. Likewise, "All things have been made through him,"[260] that is, through the Word.

70. Now, just as cooperation is understood here in that the Father and the Word are two; likewise, a simple operation is understood in that God is said to have made all things through his Word, that is, through that unity which he and his Word are. However, this must be understood about that which comes into being or which has been made; that is, about a creature, which either is made in such a way that there exists what did not exist, or around which something is made so that the creature can subsist once it has been made. Indeed, what is not made in God the Creator of all, but does exist, must in no way be considered a creature. Clearly, the Father has begotten, and this the Son does not do; the Son is begotten, and this is not done by the Father who has begotten. But this is not something created, but the essence of the divinity which makes all things. For, when "the Word was made Flesh."[261] the entire Trinity in cooperation made that which only the Word was made; namely, flesh, which, after it was made, was assumed by the Word alone in the unity of his person. Thus, the Word is said to have been made in time, because God is with God. But also, the entire Trinity made the voice of the Father which was heard over our Lord saying, "This is my beloved Son,"[262] although it was spoken by the Father alone. This is also true of the dove in which the Holy Spirit appeared over our Lord.[263] All of these were made in time; they must be considered in no other way than as they are.

71. We have said what we could about the Divine Names which are spoken about God substantially or relatively and about the relation by which Father, Son, and Holy Spirit are spoken of in relation to one another according to the propriety of these names. We have drawn whatever we have said,

260. Jn 1:3.
261. Jn 1:14.
262. Mt 3:17.
263. Mt 3:16.

not from our own fonts,[264] but from the fonts of the Savior,[265] from the Holy Scriptures, and from the thoroughly reliable testimonies of the holy Fathers;[266] we have investigated the knowledge of some things from the indications given by their names. And indeed, these names are new for men in the preaching of the faith; I mean the names, not the realities belonging to the names. For, the realities belonging to the names are not so much coeternal with God as they are God.

72. And now, what is that name of "God," or what is its source? [267] Who has imposed this name on God? A name is usually imposed on an inferior by someone who is above him. Why, therefore, is that supreme majesty called God by absolutely all men by common usage and according to the general opinion of all? This is a word which expresses the natural fear in man for the supreme essence and by it he declares in some way that that essence exists, although he wishes to declare what that essence is, but cannot. From the Greek, God is called *theos* which means "fear." This name signifies, as has been said, the natural fear of man for the supreme essence. And though man does not dare to impose a name on God; nevertheless, he in some way signifies the reality for which no name is suited, more by the use of human language than by the proper signification of a name. Consequently, when we wish to speak of him but cannot, we simply call him ineffable, as we call him invisible whom we cannot see; and thus by saying less we say more about him who surpasses all understanding[268] and comprehension.

264. Prov 5:15.
265. Is 12:3.
266. See Par. 74 below; also William's *Letter to Haymo* 10, CF 12, p. 6: "I drew what I have said from the fountains of the holy Fathers ... " William makes a similar statement of dependency on the Fathers in his Er Guil, PL 180:334BC.
267. William's source here is Isidore of Seville, *Etymologiae* 7:1. A possible source for Isidore is the work formerly attributed to Jerome, *De deo et nominibus ejus*, PL 23:1307A. In any case, the ultimate source for this etymology seems to be Servius, *Comm. in Verg. Aen.* 12:139: *quod graece δέος, latine timor vocatur, inde deus dictus est, quod omnis religio sit timoris.* For a different etymology of *deus* employed by William see his *Exposition on the Song of Songs*, CF 6, p. 124.
268. Phil 4:7.

73. Moreover, since, as has already been said above,[269] all the Divine Names are one, the name of the Lord our God must be understood to constitute a certain knowledge of him which is entrusted to the faithful to some degree by all these names. And when he wishes he reveals himself through this knowledge to whomever he wishes and as he wishes. Indeed, this is the name which we, taught by the Savior's commands and instructed by the teachings of God, pray may be sanctified daily in us by our Father who is in heaven.[270] And it is sanctified in us when, from the understanding of life which is in that name, he himself who is named is made known to us by sanctifying us; also, when in speaking of God or in praying to him he is named in the Holy Spirit by us in that manner of naming by which the Apostle says, "Lord Jesus in the Holy Spirit."[271] And also, "Whoever invokes the name of the Lord in this way will be saved."[272] And, "They place their hope in it who know this is your name."[273] And, "They glory in it who love his name."[274] And, "They desire to be judged according to the judgment of those who love his name."[275] And this is done when, for those who feel this way and invoke the name of the Lord, through the workings of grace within them, the reality of the name grows sweet in their hearts and the name savors on their lips; likewise, when the Lord is invoked who already rules in the heart of the one invoking; when the cry is made to God in the Holy Spirit, "Abba, Father,"[276] and the conscience of the one who cries out testifies that he is the Son of God.[277] And this must be understood of the other names of the Lord. Indeed, there is no name of God which according to its own form does not

269. See the first part of Par. 48 above.
270. Mt 6:9; William borrows "taught by the Savior's commands and instructed by the teachings of God" from the Roman Liturgy where it introduces the "Our Father."
271. 1 Cor 12:3.
272. Rom 10:13.
273. Cf. Ps 9:11.
274. Cf. Ps 5:12.
275. Cf. Ps 118:132.
276. Rom 8:15.
277. Cf. Rom 8:16.

breathe a similar grace upon the one who invokes it. For this is the name which in the Apocalypse[278] is promised to the conqueror of this world, written on a new stone not with an iron graver but with the finger of God. Truly, the Catholic faith is a totally smooth, rounded stone and who wishes to gnaw at it does not find a place to sink his teeth into it. On it is inscribed the new name of the Lord which faithfully renews the person who names it when he is informed by the knowledge of the spiritual form of faith in God. This occurs when faith, beginning to work through love,[279] also begins to be formed into love and through love into understanding, and through understanding into love, or into understanding and love at the same time.[280] It is difficult for a man so affected to discern which comes from which, since already in the heart of the one who believes, understands, and loves, these three are one, somewhat in the likeness of the supreme Trinity.

CONTEMPLATION OF THE MYSTERY OF THE TRINITY

74. We have now undertaken to investigate the exterior reasoning of the faith concerning the Trinity and its external expression, which, after it has been formed in our interior man,[281] will exist after the manner of that life about which we read: God first of all formed man in his image and likeness[282] and then breathed into his face the breath of life and he was made a living soul.[283] To the degree that it has been permitted and to the extent that the Lord has granted it, we have tried to treat briefly what we could touch upon concerning

278. Apoc 2:17.
279. Gal 5:6.
280. Compare William's *Exposition on the Song of Songs* 122, CF 6, p. 99, where he speaks of understanding passing into love and love into understanding. Both these passages must be seen against the background of Gregory the Great's *amor ipse notitia est,* quoted by William in Adv Abl, PL 180:252C, and developed extensively in Cant; see especially par. 57, CF 6:46 and note 18 there.
281. Rom 7:22; Eph 3:16.
282. Gen 1:26.
283. Gen 2:7.

the Divine Names, relying not on our own understanding, but that of the holy Fathers. [284] We proceed even now with fear and trembling[285] to fall prostrate and cry out, [286] Holy Trinity, in your presence, O Lord our God, you who have made us. You cause us to pray and entreat that you not permit us to err in any way in the contemplation of, or belief in, that form to which we seek to be conformed. Also, you instruct us in all the Scriptures which are about you that, just as you are three in one, so also we are to be made one in you through the power of the faith by which we believe this.

75. Thus, the form of the faith, with which everything we have said above complies, is just as we have often said already;[287] namely, that the Father is God, the Son is God and the Holy Spirit is God, and yet there are not three gods, but one God. This form of Trinity and unity allows no extension of parts through space in any direction. The Father does not locally receive the Son who remains in him; nor does the Son locally receive the Father in him; nor are the Father and Son emptied when they send forth the Holy Spirit to illuminate their whole creation. Truly, they are three, but are not separate; they are one, but are not confused; yet, although they are three, they are one; although they are one, they are three:[288] three because of the Sabellians, one because of the Arians. The Trinity itself is not in one God, but the Trinity is God; and God is not in the Trinity, but God is the Trinity itself. Indeed, God is not anything more than the Trinity, nor is the Trinity anything other than one God. Thus, when we direct our mind's eye to confess the Father, Son, and Holy Spirit, we must repell far from our minds the forms of visible things, the ages of natures which are subject to time, places where bodies are present and bodies which are present in places. Let

---

284. See the beginning of Par. 71 where William makes a similar statement about his sources.

285. 1 Cor 2:3.

286. Ps 94:6.

287. For example, see the end of Par. 28 above.

288. William borrows this sentence directly from Augustine, Ep 170:5 both here and in his *Exposition on the Epistle to the Romans* 6.

the mind be freed of what is extended in space, what is
enclosed with limits, and whatever is not always everywhere
not totally everywhere.[289]

76. In short, a concept formed about the Triune Godhead
should understand nothing as separate, should seek nothing
by degrees; and if it perceives anything worthy of God let it
not dare deny it to any of the persons. For, with every degree
of existence excluded, the substance of the Divinity in the
Trinity is one and is unchangeable; it is undivided in action,
united in will, alike in omnipotence, equal in glory, and at
the same time fills all things and contains everything. And
this must be confessed of the three persons in such a way
that the inseparable equality of the one essence preserves
unity, and the Trinity of Father, Son, and Holy Spirit admits
of no isolation. [290] Indeed, God is alone, for he is Father, Son
and Holy Spirit beyond which there is no other God; but
God the Father is not at any time alone, for he is always what
he is in relation to the Son; the Son is never alone, for he is
always in relation to the Father; the Holy Spirit is never
alone, for he is always in relation to the Father and the
Son.[291] Still, God must not be spoken of or thought of as
threefold,[292] for although he is one in three persons, nevertheless he is complete in each of these. For there, triplicity [293]
causes no obscurity nor does unity cause the persons to be
indistinguishable, because some divine number, completely
removed from every numerical difference, causes that Trinity
which is there, in such a way that the form of the simple
Godhead renders alien to it every confusion of triplicity. And
this form is nowhere unless it is there where there is a
number above number, by which three are one and one is
three.

77. And mortal man should not seek with human reason to
investigate the modality by which these things are said of

289. William borrows the previous two sentences and the first sentence of Par.
76 from Leo the Great, *Sermo* 77:4.
290. The previous two sentences are from Leo the Great, *Sermo* 76:2-3.
291. For this sentence see *De trin.* 6:9.
292. "Threefold" translates *triplex*. This is the only use of the word in the
treatise. Compare *De trin.* 6:7 where Augustine denies that God is threefold.
293. For triplicity (*triplicitas*) see Par. 65, n. 243.

God beyond human modality, since you, Lord our God, in no way and according to no modality must be thought and believed to be subject to any modality. Rather, every modality is below you, and from you from whom is whatever is or whatever is possible to be. Indeed, you and your essence are your cause and mode of existing. Therefore, because you exist in this way you are totally an unsearchable and inscrutable depth;[294] "totally," however, not that by this you are to be understood as limited in modality, but that you are to be understood, as you can be understood, as infinite. Those whom in this life you have made worthy through faith will see this in the future life by enjoying you where they will see you face to face as you are, [295] and by seeing will become as you are. For, your beloved apostle John promises this to us saying, "We will be like him, for we will see him as he is." [296] In the next life, those who will see you will no longer be deceived or fooled; their vision will no longer be doubtful, nor will their thoughts pass from one to the other, going and returning; rather, with a single glance they will perceive all their knowledge, which will be only about you, O true God. The vision of that contemplation or the contemplation of that vision[297] will not pass from the Father to the Son, from the Son to the Holy Spirit; it will not be divided into three, nor will it be gathered into one; but in a blessed perpetuity and a perpetual blessedness [298] men, no longer seeking but enjoying, will contemplate you the one true God, Father, Son, and Holy Spirit living forever and ever.

78. What the Lord says seems properly said of God the Father, "No one is good except God alone."[299] And this, "That they may know you the one true God." [300] And what the Apostle says, "Honor and glory to God alone, the immortal,

---

294. Cf. Rom 11:33.
295. 1 Cor 13:12; 1 Jn 3:2.
296. 1 Jn 3:2.
297. This turn of phrase, *visio illius contemplationis seu contemplatio illius visionis* is an example of a figure of speech called antimetabole.
298. This is another example of antimetabole.
299. Lk 18:19.
300. Jn 17:3.

invisible king of the ages."[301] Likewise, "Blessed and only sovereign King of kings and Lord of lords, who alone possesses immortality, and dwells in inaccessible light, whom no man has seen or can see."[302] But these things and others like them, which are properly spoken of God, are not proper to the Father in such a way as to be in some way less proper to the Son and the Holy Spirit. For the Father, Son, and Holy Spirit exist consubstantially; but the Father exists principally; not principally as if eminently, or with any primacy of time or dignity, but with primacy of origin.[303] God the Father is, so to speak, the font and source of divinity,[304] the principle of the Son and the Holy Spirit who are from him and have from him the being which they are. But although God the Father is the principle of the Son and the principle of the Holy Spirit, and the three are the principle of all creation; nevertheless, let no one believe the Father, Son, and Holy Spirit are three or four principles, for they are one principle just as they are one God.[305] Now, the Father must not be called the principle of the principle because the Son,

301. 1 Tim 1:17.
302. 1 Tim 6:15-16. The paragraph to here is based on *De trin.* 2:9.
303. This sentence contains an emendation of the MS with respect to one word. The Charleville MS reads *Nec enim consubstantialiter sunt Pater, Filius et Spiritus sanctus, sed principaliter Pater* etc. The Uppsala MS C. 79 also has the reading *Nec enim* on f. 91ʳ. This reading creates a theological problem in that William seems to deny the consubstantiality of the Persons in the Trinity. This in itself makes the MS reading suspect. I have emended the *Nec enim* to read *Etenim*. Internal evidence in support of this emendation can be found in William's earlier statements in the treatise about consubstantiality: he speaks of "consubstantial unity" in Par. 46 and "that nature of the consubstantial Trinity" in Par. 68. See also Pars. 11 and 44. The most important passage in the treatise in support of the emendation is in Par. 68. Compare that paragraph with William's statements here. External support for the emendation comes from the PL reading which is *Etenim* (PL 180:435D). Migne's text is a reprint of Tissier's edition published in *Bibliotheca patrum cisterciensium* (Bonne–Fontaine, 1662) Tome 4. The Tissier reading is also *Etenim.* Adam, *op. cit.,* says that Tissier made use of a MS from Signy for his edition of William's works. Furthermore, Adam speculates that this MS may very well have been Charleville 114. It might be noted that Davy's edition of the *Enigma* contains the reading *Nec enim* but without any note or comment on the theological problem this causes.
304. See Par. 68 above where the Father is called the source of divinity.
305. See *De trin.* 5:13-14 for the discussion of the three Persons as a single principle.

whose principle he is, is with him the principle of the Holy
Spirit, rather, in the Trinity principle must be understood
from principle just as God from God. There is one God, one
principle: the Father of the Son, and with the Son of the
Holy Spirit, and with the Son and the Holy Spirit of all
creation. Indeed, we pray to God the Father, and we adore
him and always give thanks to him, not without the Son and
the Holy Spirit. Still, this is "through the Son," just as
through the mediator of God and man, our Lord Jesus
Christ;[306] and "in the Holy Spirit" our Paraclete and the
advocate of our prayers before God, [307] without whom we do
not know how to pray as we ought, nor are we heard when
we pray. [308] Now, when we pray to the Father through the
Son in the Holy Spirit, [309] just as to one through the other in
another, we pray to only one God differing in nothing from
God; but we have confidence in God to whom we pray, not
as if from ourselves but from the justice which is through the
faith of our Lord Jesus Christ. [310] And we become worthy to
be heard through the grace of the Holy Spirit consoling us
and giving us life interiorly.[311]

79. It is said about the Son, "In the beginning was the
Word and the Word was with God, and the Word was
God."[312] When it says here "was . . . was . . . was" about that
which always is, it must be understood first of all that it does
not matter how times are spoken of with reference to God,
since there is no time which fittingly expresses what is
spoken about, namely, eternity. When it says here, "In the
beginning was the Word," the coeternity of the Father and
the Son is indicated; through the statement "the Word was
with God" is indicated the truth of the persons; through "the
Word was God" is indicated the consubstantiality of the

306. 1 Tim 2:5.
307. 1 Jn 2:1.
308. Rom 8:26. For the formula "through the Son in the Holy Spirit" see Par.
69. Also, see Brooke, "The Speculative Development" p. 207, n. 77 for a discussion of this formula with reference to the Trinitarian life *ad intra* and *ad extra*.
309. Cf. Rom 11:36.
310. 2 Cor 3:4-5.
311. Cf. Rom 8:26.
312. Jn 1:1.

Word with the one speaking. Also, the Son is said to be from the Father, and this is the divine birth; the eternal Son is said to be from the eternal Father, and this is the eternity of the divine birth. And he is born, and the Son of God must be understood as born always: "born" lest in any way that birth be thought imperfect; "always" so that the eternity of that birth might proclaim itself. For, "born" pertains to perfection, "always" pertains to eternity, so that in some way that essence without time can be designated with temporal language. He is Son because truly he is born, God from God, by a true but divine, inscrutable and ineffable birth. "For who will explain his generation? " [313] But we do not shrink from preaching the true name of the generation and birth in God, like the Manicheans or certain Arians who say that the Son of God is a creature; but we believe and we profess that he is born God from God, and that there is one who has begotten and who is begotten.

80. However, just as the Son is called the Son of one who begets, so he is called the Word of one who speaks, in order that somehow in many ways what can in no way be explained might be spoken of. For the Word of God by a great and hidden mystery bears the name of a human word among men, and some similarity to it. For, there is in man in the depths of his heart some word concerning every reality, some conception of truth, without a voice, without syllables, without any form. For, just as a man's word in some way is made a voice by assuming a voice so that it can be manifested to the senses of men, so "the Word was made flesh" [314] by assuming that in which it could be manifested to men. And just as a man's word is made a voice and not changed into a voice, so the Word of God was made flesh; but let it be far removed from the belief of all the faithful that this Word was changed into flesh. [315]

---

313. Is 53:8. The ineffable generation of the Son is a point about which William leveled criticism against William of Conches, who had said that this verse speaks only of the difficulty, not the impossibility, of explaining the Son's generation from the Father; see PL 180:333D.

314. Jn 1:14.

315. These last two sentences are practically verbatim from *De trin.* 15:11.

81. And the Word of God made flesh has been made for us a word not of human instruction, but divine, teaching us in brief to fulfill all the law saying, "You shall love the Lord your God with your whole heart and your whole soul and your whole mind; and your neighbor as yourself."[316] Then he says, "On these two commandments the whole law and the prophets depend." [317] Then, his whole life on earth, through the humanity which he condescended to assume, was an instruction and teaching of morals. Riches, honors, pleasures, and everything which we wrongly desire to have in our lifetime he showed to be of no value by doing without them and by his teaching; poverty, reproaches, injuries, sorrows, and bodily death and everything which men wish to avoid and which commonly cause men to turn away from zeal for living well, he made powerless by bearing patiently.[318] Indeed, he taught carnal men, given over to thoughts of the flesh and unable to behold the truth with their minds, what a lofty place among creatures human nature held, because by assuming humanity the Word of God was made a single person from two natures. [319]

82. Now, it is about this that the Prophet says, "He sent his word and healed them; and he delivered them from their destruction."[320] However, in this mission two things must be pondered very carefully, namely, that the mission of the Son from the Father be understood neither as separable nor temporal. Now, since it was brought about by the Father and the Son that the Son appeared in the flesh, he who appeared in the flesh is fittingly said to have been sent, and he who did not appear in the flesh to have sent, because those things which take place exteriorly before our bodily eyes proceed from an interior spiritual preparation, and therefore are fittingly said to have been sent. [321] Moreover, the form of that

316. Lk 10:27.
317. Mt 22:40.
318. The previous two sentences are a paraphrase of a passage William borrows from *De vera rel.* 16:31 and uses here and in Par. 12 above.
319. This sentence is substantially a rewording of a sentence borrowed from *De vera rel.* 16:30 and used in Par. 11 above.
320. Ps 106:20.
321. This sentence and the remainder of Par. 82 are taken from *De trin.* 2:5.

humanity which was assumed belongs only to the Son, and not also to the Father. Wherefore, the invisible Father, together with the Son who is invisible with him, by making that same Son visible is said to have sent him. If he became visible in such a way that he ceased to be invisible with the Father; that is, if the substance of the invisible Word were changed, passing into the visible creature, the Son would be understood as sent by the Father in such a way that he would be only "sent" and not "sending." Indeed, since the form of a servant [322] was taken in such wise that the form of God remained unchangeable, it is clear that what appeared in the Son was made by the invisible Father and by the invisible Son and by the invisible Holy Spirit; that is, that the Son himself was sent as visible by those who were invisible.

83. Truly, the whole Trinity made the servant's form which the only-begotten God assumed; but although in this form there is the operation of the whole Trinity, nevertheless, the reception of it belongs to the Son alone, not to the whole Trinity. But if in Christ the nature of the divinity and of the flesh were made one, the Incarnation could as a consequence be believed proper to the whole Trinity. But in Christ there is one nature which the Only-begotten of God possesses, indeed, inseparably with the Father and the Holy Spirit; in addition, he has his own unique humanity with which his divinity possesses not one nature, but one person.

84. But neither should the mission of the Word be believed temporal; although in the Word himself, in the very Wisdom of God, from eternity without time there was a time in which it was fitting for him to appear in the flesh. And when this fulness of time had come, [323] God is said to have sent his Son in such a way that since he was God and man, just as he was born in both natures, so he might die in both natures, not through constraint but freely. For, the Divinity suffered in the flesh everything which was of the flesh, because God assumed flesh, capable of suffering, together with human

322. Phil 2:7.
323. Gal 4:4.

affections. However, the Divinity did not share suffering with the flesh, because the Divinity remained always in its nature incapable of suffering. Indeed, the same person was God and man.

85. Now, this must be discerned and held with the most certain faith; for, just as in the Trinity which is God we confess three persons and one nature, so in the Lord Jesus Christ we must understand two natures and one person. And just as three persons must be believed inseparable in the nature of the Divinity, so in the person of Christ must two natures be believed inseparable. Thus we believe the Son of God is begotten from the substance of the Father, God from God, without any beginning to his birth; he is not begotten from nothing, because he is from the Father; he is not just called this, but possesses the name from the truth of his nature. For what does it profit the Son that he be called by the name of Only-begotten if he is deprived of the truth of the name?[324] For, in vain is he called the Only-begotten if in his birth is predicated not the truth of his nature from God who gives birth to him, but the bounty of the one who gives. And to others, as many as received him, he gave the power to become sons of God.[325] But in that mystery of eternal birth the eternal and unchangeable Father begot another who was not different from him; and as much as he brought forth in begetting, so much did he himself remain. He distinguished from himself in person one whom in nature he has completely in himself.

86. Thus the ineffable Son, born without a beginning from the Father, came whole and entire into the womb of the Virgin after the fulness of time had come,[326] so that sent by the Father he might be made from a woman. Reigning whole and entire in the bosom of the Father,[327] he formed himself

324. The previous two sentences are taken from Augustine; the exact reference is unknown. William uses this passage in his Er Guil, PL 180:338A and attributes it to Augustine.
325. Jn 1:12.
326. Gal 4:4.
327. Jn 1:18.

whole and entire in the bosom of his mother. Part of him did not remain in the Father and part come into the Virgin, since whole and entire he remained in the Father that which he was; and whole and entire in the Virgin he became what he was not. Thus the true and supreme God took into himself a complete human nature; and thus with the truth of the divine and the human substance remaining without confusion, the fulness of the Divinity[328] joined itself with a full human nature, so that henceforth with the unity of the person remaining, neither the man Christ could be separated from his divinity, nor could the same Christ God be separated from his humanity. Now, this inseparable unity of the person in whom Christ is born God and man causes the man Christ to be born from God through grace, with the exception of the truth and fulness of his human nature, and the same Christ God to suffer willingly in the flesh, with the exception of the fulness of the divine substance which is incapable of suffering. Therefore, we confess that the divinity of Christ, which Holy Scripture declares to be unchangeable, suffered in the flesh such that, nevertheless, we believe that it did not share in suffering with the flesh. Thus, God suffered in the flesh because he assumed flesh capable of suffering. However, he did not share the suffering of the flesh, because while suffering in the flesh the divine nature remained incapable of suffering.

87. "God is spirit,"[329] says the Lord. The Father is spirit, the Son is spirit, and he who is called Holy Spirit is spirit; and still there are not three spirits, but one Spirit of whom the Lord says that "God is spirit," just as there are not three gods, but one God. Now, although each of them is spirit, and certainly each is holy, the Holy Spirit, who is common to both, is properly designated by that name which is common to both, and just as he is something common to both, he is whatever is common to them: their divinity, love, sweetness, blessedness, and so forth.

328. Col 2:9.
329. Jn 4:24. This entire paragraph is reminiscent of a similar passage in *De trin.* 5:11. For the Holy Spirit as that which is common to both Father and Son see *De trin.* 6:5.

88. Just as the Son is from the Father by birth, so also the Holy Spirit is from the Father and the Son by procession, but principally from the Father, since it has been given to the Son through his birth from the Father that the Holy Spirit is equally from him and from the Father by procession. Indeed, by birth the Son receives from the Father the fact that he is God from God, and one God with the Father. Nevertheless, the reasoning of faith does not permit this process to be reversed with reference to the Son; namely, that since in a similar way the Father and the Holy Spirit are one God, also in a similar way the Son can be understood as being equally from the Holy Spirit and the Father. For the nativity of the one Son from two fathers would constitute a confusion of the Trinity, and this is completely alien to the reasoning of faith. Therefore, since the Holy Spirit is the Spirit of the Father and the Son, and proceeds from both, and is the love and unity of both, it is clear that he cannot be one of the two, for it is by him that each is united, by him that the Begotten is loved by the Begetter and loves his Begetter. And thus it is clear that they exist not through participation in another but by their own essence, and not by the gift of the other but by the gift of themselves do they maintain the unity of the Spirit in the bond of peace. [330]

89. Now in the procession by which the Holy Spirit is said to proceed from the Father and the Son, his divine coessence with them is understood. However, because he also proceeds into creation he is declared to be the gift of God. [331] The Holy Spirit is so truly the gift of God that of the gifts of God of which no one possesses all, no one can possess any who does not possess the Holy Spirit. And whoever possesses any of these gifts possesses them only in the Holy Spirit. Although many gifts are given through the Holy Spirit, without love, without which they are nothing, they profit nothing. [332] For the Holy Spirit is not properly called the gift unless it is

330. Eph 4:3. These last few lines are a paraphrase of *De trin.* 6:5.
331. This paragraph is almost entirely a cento of passages drawn from *De trin.* 15:18.
332. 1 Cor 13:3.

because of love about which it is said: "The love of God is poured out in our hearts through the Holy Spirit who has been given to us."[333] Nothing is more excellent than this gift which alone separates the sons of the kingdom from the sons of perdition,[334] and alone leads to the kingdom even if other gifts are not possessed. For even faith itself can in some way be without love, but cannot be beneficial. For faith is beneficial only when it operates through love.[335] Now the Holy Spirit is the love of the Father and the Son, by which they love one another, and the unity by which they are one. Whenever he is given to a man he enkindles him with love for God and neighbor. And he himself is that love, because God is love;[336] and a man has no ability to love God unless it is given by God.[337]

90. Thus, indeed, it is said, "because God loved us first";[338] and we, therefore, love him because he loved us first. Now God loved us first, not with an affective love but an effective love,[339] since before the ages he predestined us to be adopted sons[340] and in the time of his good pleasure[341] he poured out his love in our hearts through the Holy Spirit.[342] For, the Eternal loves no one temporally, and he who is unchangeable is not subject to affections. The Spirit of the Lord fills the earth[343] with the goodness of his omnipotence, and bathes all things in the great richness of his superabundant grace[344] according to the capacity and measure of each, so that each might take its proper place and willingly remain there. He

333. Rom 5:5.
334. Cf Jn 17:12.
335. Gal 5:6.
336. 1 Jn 4:8.
337. These last two sentences are from *De trin.* 15:17.
338. 1 Jn 4:19.
339. For this distinction between affective and effective love see *On Contemplating God* 11, CF 3, p. 58 and n. 138.
340. Eph 1:5.
341. Ps 68:14.
342. Rom 5:5.
343. Wisdom 1:7.
344. For the phrase "superabundant grace" see Rom 5:20. This sentence from "and bathes all things in the great richness . . . " is taken from *De trin.* 6:10. William also uses it in his *Exposition on the Epistle to the Romans* 7.

bestows goods, disposes what is beneficial, and distributes to the pious and the faithful different kinds of gifts.[345] And to the impious and the unfaithful he often gives peaceful times, bodily health, material prosperity, the abundance which comes from the dew of heaven and the richness of the earth,[346] and things similar to these. And the Spirit sometimes takes these same things away from the holy to test their holiness, and gives them to wicked sinners to challenge and build up their charity. For the sons of grace[347] and the poor in spirit[348] he is the advocate and consoler in the exile of the present life; he is strength against adversities, help in tribulations. He himself, teaching man to pray as he ought and drawing man to God and rendering him pleasing and able to be heard,[349] illumines his intellect and shapes his disposition. The Spirit creates and brings to perfection and is sufficient alone, if he can exist alone or ought to be spoken of as alone. But he is sufficient alone because he cannot be separated from the Father and the Son inseparably together with whom he does all that he does.[350]

345. 1 Cor 12:4.
346. Gen 27:28.
347. Eph 1:5-6.
348. Mt 5:3.
349. Jn 14:26; Rom 8:26.
350. This sentence is substantially that of Augustine in *De trin.* 1:8.

SELECTED BIBLIOGRAPHY

TEXTS AND TRANSLATIONS OF THE *ENIGMA OF FAITH*:

Anderson, John D., *The Enigma fidei of William of Saint Thierry, a Translation and Commentary* (Washington D.C., 1971).
Davy, M.-M., *Deux traités sur la foi: Le Miroir de la foi, L'Enigme de la foi* (Paris, 1959).
Migne, J. P., *Patrologia latina*, vol. 180 (Paris, 1885) cols. 397-440.
Tissier, Bertrand, *Bibliotheca patrum cisterciensium*, vol. 4 (Bonnefontaine, 1662) pp. 93-112.

WORKS CONCERNING THE *ENIGMA OF FAITH*:

Adam, André, *Guillaume de Saint-Thierry sa vie et ses oeuvres* (Bourg, 1923).
Brooke, Odo, "The Speculative Development of the Trinitarian Theology of William of St. Thierry in the *Aenigma fidei,*" RTAM 27 (1960) pp. 193-211 and vol. 28 (1961) pp. 26-58.
—————, "The Trinitarian Aspect of the Ascent of the Soul to God in the Theology of William of St Thierry," RTAM 26 (1959) pp. 85-127.
Ceglar, Stanislaus, *William of Saint Thierry the Chronology of His Life With a Study of His Treatise* On the Nature of Love, *His Authorship of the* Brevis commentatio, *the* In lacu, *and the* Reply to Cardinal Matthew (Washington, D.C., 1971).
Davy, Marie-Madeleine, *Théologie et mystique de Guillaume de Saint-Thierry* (Paris, 1954).
Déchanet, Jean-Marie, "L'amitié d'Abélard et de Guillaume de Saint-Thierry," *Revue d'histoire ecclésiastique* 35 (1939) pp. 761-774.
—————, *Aux sources de la spiritualité de Guillaume de Saint-Thierry* (Bruges, 1940).
—————, "Guillaume de Saint-Thierry," *Dictionnaire de spiritualité ascétique et mystique*, vol. 6 (Paris, 1965) pp. 1241-1263.

————, *Guillaume de Saint-Thierry l'homme et son oeuvre* (Bruges, 1942). Translated by Richard Strachan as *William of St Thierry, the Man and his Work*, CS 10 (Spencer, 1972).

————, "Un recueil singulier d'opuscules de Guillaume de Saint-Thierry: Charleville 114," *Scriptorium* 6 (1952) pp. 196-212.

Delisle, Leopold, "Manuscrits legués à la Bibliothèque Nationale par Armand Durand," *Bibliothèque de l'Ecole des Chartes* 55 (1894) pp. 627-660; article includes *Appendix*: "Chronique de l'abbaye de Signy" pp. 644-660.

Hourlier, Jacques, "Guillaume de Saint-Thierry et la *Brevis commentatio in cantica,*" *Analecta sacri ordinis cisterciensis* 12 (1956) pp. 105-114.

Poncelet, Albert, "Vie ancienne de Guillaume de Saint-Thierry," *Mélanges Godefroid Kurth* vol. 1 (Paris, 1908) pp. 85-96.

Wilmart, André, "La série et la date des ouvrages de Guillaume de Saint-Thierry," *Revue Mabillon* 14 (1924) pp. 157-167.

————, "Un conjecture mal fondée au sujet des Sentences de Guillaume de Saint-Thierry," *Revue bénédictine* 35 (1923) pp. 263-267.

INDEX

The references are to the paragraphs of the *Enigma of Faith.*

121

CISTERCIAN STUDIES SERIES

Under the direction of the same Board of Editors as the *Cistercian Fathers Series*, the *Cistercian Studies Series* seeks to make available to the English-speaking world significant studies produced in other languages, as well as various monastic texts and studies of perennial value with a view to placing the Cistercian Fathers in their full historical context and to bring out their present day relevance.

CISTERCIAN PUBLICATIONS
CONSORTIUM PRESS
Washington, D.C.
1974